LAND MAMMALS OF ALASKA

A FIELD GUIDE FOR CHILDREN

The I Saw It! Series #1: Field Guides, Journals, and Coloring Books for Children

by

Barbara L. Brovelli-Moon

Artwork by Kimberly A. Sherry

Junior Naturalist:________________________________ **Date:**________________________________

ANCHORAGE, ALASKA

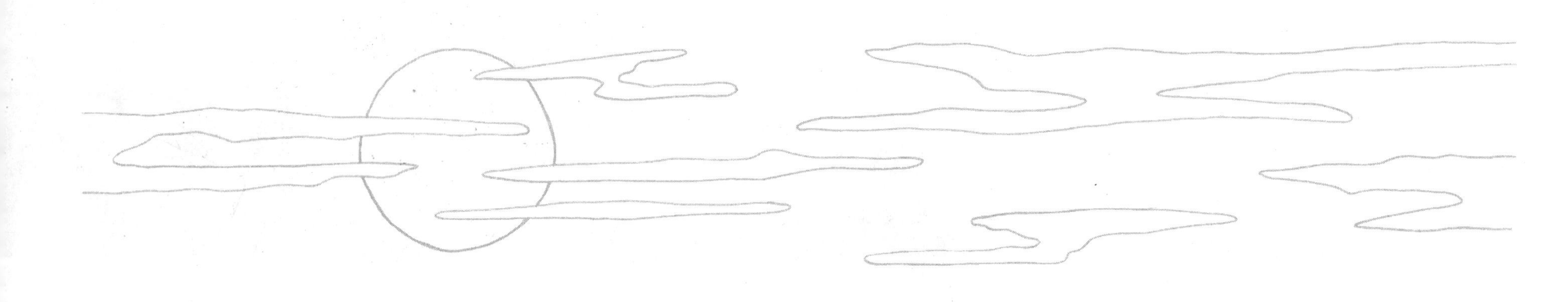

Brovelli-Moon, Barbara (Illustrator, Kim Sherry)

Land Mammals of Alaska: A Field Guide for Children
The I Saw It! Series #1: Field Guides, Journals, and Coloring Books for Children

ISBN: 978-0-9962559-2-9

Published by OceanOtter Publishing

Designed by Phillip Gessert

Edited by Norma Neill and Amy Frackman

Printed in the United States of America

10 9 8 7 6 5 4 3 2 1

Contact the author at oceanotterpublishing@gmail.com or www.oceanotterpublishing.com

See more of Kim Sherry's art work at www.kimsherrygallery.com

Table of Contents And Checklist of Sightings

In Memoriam

Allan A. Trefry, mentor and friend. Thank you for sharing your love of music, *The Life of Pi*, and for teaching me to live life fully. You are missed by so many.

Vince Correa, who left Kara and Eric far too soon. You are deeply missed.

James Verhaeghe II, an amazing student who taught us all so much.

Madeline and Millie, my canine companions, who saw so many of Alaska's mammals with me.

Acknowledgements

Thanks, Mike Kemmer, for the idea. Kim Sherry, the drawings are exactly what I wanted. Amy Frackman, thanks for ongoing tech help, reading, and rounding up sixth graders to edit—you're amazing. Norma Neill and Linda Wichman, thanks for the painstaking, last-minute editing. Sakura Likar, Sandy Pendergast, Carol Dickason, Linda Hawkins, and Maureen Jones, thanks for reading and making suggestions. Brayden and Brennen Battle of Battleboys' Graphics, thank you for your terrific coloring , and Laila Moore, you are a great artist! Isabel Jones, Maya and Sophie Sherry, and McNeeley and Maudie Mae Olson, you are great kid editors! The glossary search kids at Northern Lights ABC School in Anchorage, Alaska—Yael, Sonja, Losi, Zayn, Sharon, Maisha, Shreya, Ashlieyh, Ashley, Riley, Ariana, and Amaret—you did great work. Jeanette Troup, Kelly Fisher, and Jim Barr, thanks for your varied ideas. Gene Dickason, thanks for the use of some of your great photographs. And Greg, what a ride we decided to take. Thanks for being at my side.

Special thanks to the Alaska Department of Fish and Game for allowing me to use information from your website, including the maps showing where the mammals live. Additionally, special thanks to Marcella Asicksik, Language Project Coordinator at the Alaska Native Heritage Center, who provided many of the Native name translations. Your assistance is greatly appreciated.

Cover photograph by Grandpa Greg Jefferies

Back cover drawing colored by Grandson Brayden Battle

Introduction

Hello, and welcome to the world of mammals. What is a mammal, you ask? A mammal is an animal who *has a backbone, lungs to breathe air, grows hair or fur on its body*, and *gives birth to live babies who drink milk from their mother.*

This book, *Land Mammals of Alaska for Children*, is . . .

. . . a field guide in which thirty-five land mammals tell their own stories. You will learn where they live, what they eat, how they act, and so much more.

. . . a journal that gives you a place to write your own story about seeing these mammals. Where were you? Who was with you? What happened? Keep a record of your experiences as you see these amazing creatures.

. . . a coloring book for you to color the images of each mammal. Follow the descriptions given to color them accurately, or color them pink, green, orange, or purple. This is your book to use as you choose.

The book also includes a checklist to record when you see one of the mammals, names for the mammals in some of the Alaska Native languages, tips on how to be safe around bears and moose, an explanation of the difference between common and scientific names, a chart of names for the males, females, offspring, and groups of a species, a glossary, and other hidden surprises! And if you want to meet some interesting marine mammals, pick up a copy of *Marine Mammals of Alaska for Children* and read their stories, too.

Enjoy getting to know the amazing land mammals of Alaska!

Why Do We All Have Three Names?

Hi. Worthington Wolf here. Every mammal in this book has three names listed at the top of its story page. Why do we all have three names? Let me explain by telling you about my names, which are . . .

Gray Wolf
Kaganaq in Alutiiq • *Canus lupus*

The first name listed is my common or popular name used by English-speaking people. That name is **Gray Wolf**. The second name listed is my common or popular name in one of the Alaska Native languages. I am known as **Kaganaq** in the Alutiiq language. My name is capitalized in this Native language, but sometimes Native names are not capitalized. All the mammals in this book have an English common name along with their name in one of the many Native languages.

The third name listed is my scientific name, ***Canus lupus.*** Everything living on our planet has a scientific name created by scientists. These complicated names are used to be absolutely positive about the identity of the life form being discussed or studied. Seven classifications, or divisions, make up my long scientific name:

Kingdom, **Phylum**, **Class**, **Order**, **Family**, **Genus**, and **Species**

("**K**ids **P**refer **C**andy **O**ver **F**resh **G**reen **S**alad" will help you remember!)

Kingdom is the largest classification, and each division after that becomes more and more specific. My entire scientific name is below, with a few of the characteristics that describe each classification.

Classification	Name	Characteristics
Kingdom	Animalia	Animal
Phylum	Chordata	Vertebrate (an animal with a backbone)
Class	Mammalian	Mammal
Order	Carnivora	Meat-eater
Family	Canidae	All dogs, wolves, jackals, foxes, and coyotes
Genus	*Canis*	Dogs, wolves, and jackals only
Species	*lupus*	Gray wolf

Everyone's scientific name is based on a Latin or Greek root. "Animalia" comes from the Latin root "animale," and "mammalian" comes from the Latin root "mammalis." Many English words come from these same roots, like the words animal and mammal. Scientific names are so long, scientists use only the last two categories, genus and species, when they talk about me, or any other life form. So in this book, the third name, written in Latin, is my genus and species. Now you know!

Male, Female, Baby, and Group Names

Mammal	*Male*	*Female*	*Baby*	*Group*
bat	—	—	pup	colony, cloud
bear	boar	sow, she-bear	cub	sleuth, sloth
beaver	—	—	pup, kit, kitten	family, colony
bison, elk	bull	cow	calf	herd, gang
caribou	—	—	calf	herd
coyote	dog	bitch	cub, pup, whelp	band, pack
deer	buck, stag	doe, cow	fawn, calf	bunch, herd
ermine or short-tailed weasel	buck, jack, dog	doe, jill	pup, kit	sneak, gang
fox	tod, dog	vixen	cub, kit, pup	leash, skulk
goat	billy, buck	nanny, doe	kid	tribe, trip, herd
hare	buck, jack	doe, jill	leveret	down, husk
lemming, muskrat, pika, vole, wolverine	—	—	—	—
lynx	—	—	kittens	—
marmot	—	—	—	colony
marten	—	—	—	richness
mink	boar	sow	cub, kit	—
moose	bull	cow	calf	herd
muskox	bull, steer	cow	calf	team, drove
otter	boar	sow	pup, whelp	bevy, lodge
porcupine	boar	sow	pup	prickle
dall sheep	ram, buck	ewe, dam	lamb, cosset	drift, flock
shrew	boar	sow	shrewlet	colony, drove
squirrel	buck	doe	pup, kit	squad, dray
wolf	dog	she-wolf	cub, pup, whelp	pack, rout
wolverine	wolverine	angeline	kit, whelp	pack
woodchuck	boar	sow	pup	town

Little Brown Bat

Keneryaq in Sugpiaq • Myotis lucifugus

Well, hello! I'm Barney Bat, a tiny mammal and the only one who can fly. There are six species of bats in Alaska, and I am the most common of all. Even though I live in more parts of this great state than my cousins, you are going to have to be very alert to find me. Know why? During the day, when you are awake and outside, I'm asleep, or roosting, in a cave, hollow tree, or abandoned building. I'm nocturnal (nock-TUR-nul), which means I only go out at night to hunt and to look around. It's very difficult to see me in the darkness with my dark, chocolate brown fur. It's also hard to see me because I zoom through the air in crazy, erratic patterns. I am able to fly faster than twenty miles per hour, though my cruising speed in usually about half that fast. I never have a flight plan, either. I just zip one way, then another, and then back a different way. I dart above trees, out over bodies of water like ponds, lakes, sloughs, slow-moving streams, and rivers, looking for a tasty, flying insect.

Are you wondering how I do all that darting around without crashing into something? Or how I actually find tiny insects in the dark? Very simply, I use echolocation (EK-o-lo-CAY-shun), which means I send out high, squeaky sounds that bounce off trees, insects, and anything else nearby. The sounds bounce back to me, and when I hear them, I sense what objects are near. I don't crash, and I find plenty to eat.

Speaking of ears, you should see mine. They are big enough that when I flop them forward, they touch the end of my nose. You probably can't do that, but there is something you might want to do. I have a secret that scientists haven't been able to solve, so maybe you would like to help them! From September to April or May, no one knows where I go. Do I fly hundreds of miles south to get away from the cold winter? Or maybe I hibernate in caves in Alaska. Do I hibernate, or just become torpid (TOR-pid), meaning asleep but able to wake up when it's above freezing? Where do I go, and what do I do? That's my secret. Ha-ha! So try to find me, and maybe I will tell you the answer!

My Facts

SIZE:
Body: 4–5 inches long, 6–8 inches from wingtip to wingtip; weight, 0.25–0.33 ounce (more than a nickel, less than a half-dollar)

COLOR:
Back: tan to chocolate-brown
Tips of hair: glossy black
Belly: tannish to pale gray

FOOD:
Insectivorous: moths, mosquitoes, other flying insects, spiders

DANGERS:
Mice, martens, snakes, hawks, weasels, owls, raccoons, cats

YEARS I LIVE:
10–30 years

Did You See Me? Tell Your Story! ____________________

____

____

____

DID YOU KNOW? Have you ever heard the simile, "He is as blind as a bat?" Don't believe it. I see very well, especially in light that is not too bright. My eyesight makes hunting at night perfect for me.

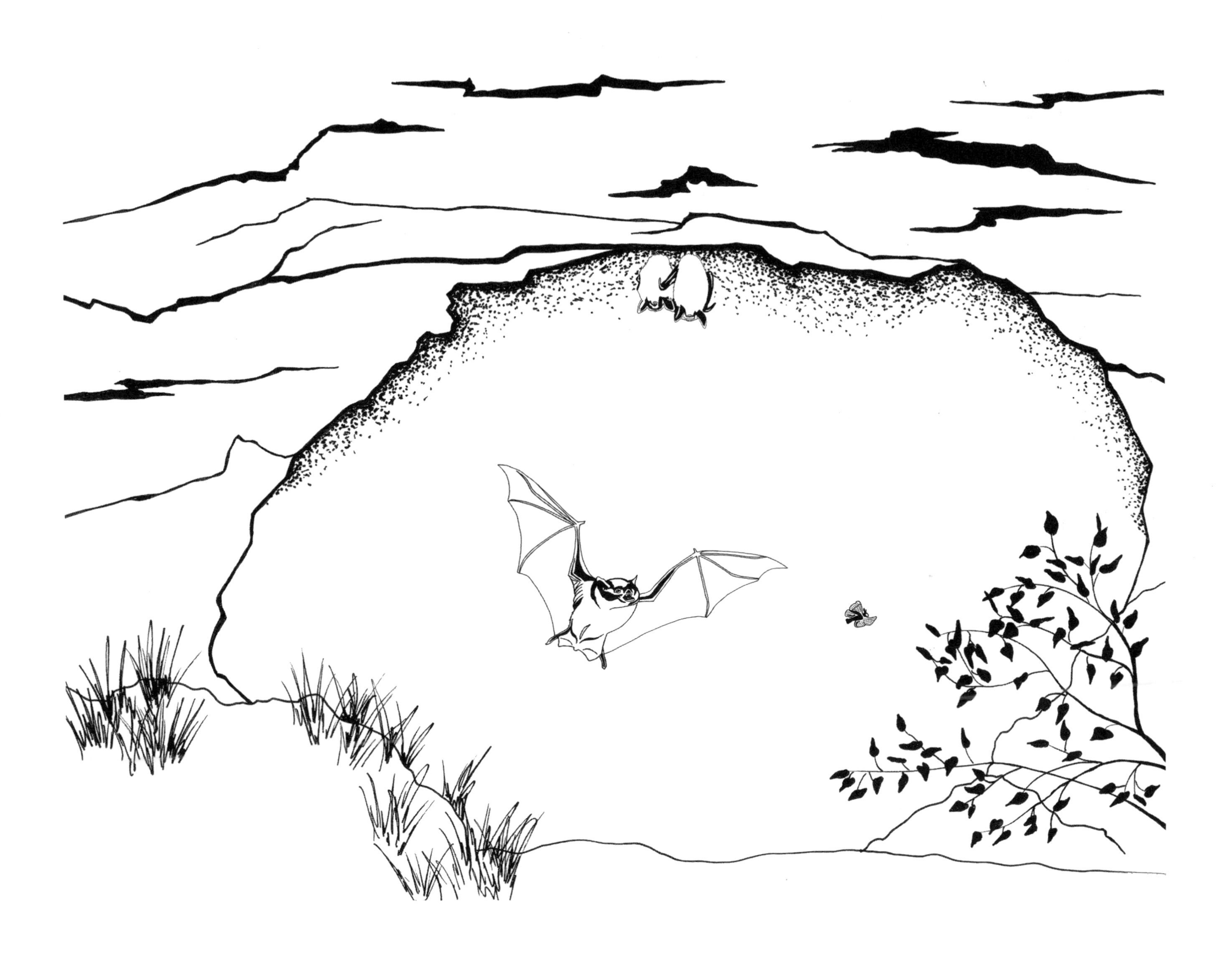

Black Bear

tungulzria in Yupik • *Ursus americanus*

Hi kids. I'm Beatrice Black Bear, smallest of all the bears. I may be little, but there are more of me than any of my brown and grizzly cousins. I live in more places than they do, too. I like open forests the best, but I also hang out in the alpine meadows in the summer, then go to lower beach or tundra areas when the mountains get chilly. And I love my excursions (ek-SKER-shuns) to town to shop for food in your garbage can. I am free to roam and eat anytime in the forest, but near humans, I make my trips at nighttime for my own safety. And though you don't want to come close to me, I probably won't hurt you. I am pretty shy. In fact, when something scares me, the first thing I do is move away with my shuffling gait, my odd way of walking, as fast as possible. If I *really* need to scram, though, I gallop away as fast as thirty-five miles per hour. And if things are totally scary, I dash to the nearest tree and climb quickly up into the branches.

See my twin cubs up in that tree? I taught them to climb at a very young age. Our short, narrow, front claws are perfect for scurrying up trees, since the curved tips make digging into the bark easy.

I don't have to worry about hiding in the wintertime, though, because I go to sleep in my den, which is usually a cozy cave in a rocky cliff. Some of my relatives sleep under fallen trees or in hollow logs, or even in huge holes under tree roots. While I'm asleep, my body goes into "dormancy," (DOOR-man-cee) which means my heart rate slows down at least seventy-five percent (instead of fifty-five beats per minute, it only beats about fourteen times). My body heat may drop as much as seven degrees. I really chill out! But if I am disturbed while I'm sleeping, I wake up super fast, and I am not happy nor friendly. Be aware, too, that if you wake me up, I may not see you because my eyes aren't very good, but I hear and smell just fine. So keep your distance, and give me my space. Or better yet, just let me sleep! That way we'll both be safe and satisfied.

My Facts

SIZE:
Boar: body, 4–6 feet long, 2.5–3.5 feet tall at shoulder; weight, 200–600 pounds at the end of summer, 30 percent less at the end of winter
Sow: 20–30 percent smaller than boar

COLOR:
Body: usually jet-black (some are brown or bluish)
Chest patch: small and white

FOOD:
Omnivorous (about 80 percent vegetation, 20 percent meat): nuts, berries, plants, carrion, fish, small or young mammals, trash

DANGERS:
Brown and grizzly bears, humans

YEARS I LIVE:
20–25 years

Did You See Me? Tell Your Story! ______________________

____

____

____

DID YOU KNOW? In the western parts of Alaska, some of us are called "cinnamon" bears because we are a rich, cinnamon color. In Southeast, some of us are called "glacier" or blue bears because of the pale bluish cast to our fur.

Brown Bear: Coastal

Masgm'ol in Sm'algyax • Ursus arctos middendorffi

Grrrr! I'm Brayden Brown Bear, the largest bear and land omnivore (OM-ni-vor) anywhere on the planet! I have several names, including brownie, big brownie, and Kodiak brown bear. Notice that "grizzly" isn't one of my names? Brennen Grizzly Bear and I are closely related brown bears, but we have our differences. I'm about one-third larger than he is, have smaller front claws, am darker in color, and prefer to live in a different area. Brennen Grizzly likes the interior, northern parts of the state. Me? I'm a coastal guy. I love the mild temperatures, beautiful forests, and open country near the sea. I find delicious plants to eat, and a huge variety of protein or meat sources. You'll find me within forty miles of the ocean and on some of the southern islands, like Kodiak Island.

Because it's warmer along the coast, I don't have to waste as much of the winter sleeping in my den as Brennen does. His inland winters are unbelievably cold and long, so he sleeps for months. While he's asleep, I roam and eat. It's no wonder I'm bigger! Plants, berries, dead whales, and seals washed up on the beach . . . You name it, and I try it. But can you guess my favorite? You're right if you said SALMON! When these fish swim up the rivers to spawn in the summer, I'm right there snagging all I can. I devour their delicious, oil-rich flesh, eggs, and brains. Unfortunately, though, there is a down-side to this fishing experience. I'm a loner and want to be by myself while I am fishing, just like all the other brownies. So when we are all fishing the same river, it can be a mess. Fighting, growling and threatening "talk," chasing . . . You wouldn't believe what goes on! The biggest and oldest bears get very bossy and crabby if I take their favorite place to fish. Or if Bertha comes around, all the young sows run for the hills. Bertha doesn't like other girls! And old Bruno? We ALL take off when he shows up. It's just how it is. Fishing can get nasty and crazy, but somehow, most of us get our fill. (Some of the youngest just don't get enough chances to fish, though, so they don't fill up for the winter.) Now, if you'll excuse me, I need to catch some of these delicious fish! Wave if you see me, but from a *very* safe distance!

My Facts

SIZE:
Boar: body, 7–9 feet long, 4 feet tall at shoulder; weight, 800–1,500 pounds at the end of summer, 25 percent less at the end of winter
Sow: 30 percent smaller than boar

COLOR:
Body: dark brown to blond
Hair: white tipped

FOOD:
Omnivorous (about 70 percent vegetation, 30 percent meat): plants, sedges, berries and other fruits, salmon, small mammals, and carrion

DANGERS:
Killer whales, sharks, humans

YEARS I LIVE:
25 years

I live in southern, highlighted, coastal areas only.

Did You See Me? Tell Your Story! ______________________________

____

____

____

DID YOU KNOW? Swimming and fishing come as naturally to me as walking on land. I easily run and swim in water, chasing salmon as they head up-river to spawn. You might even see me playing in the water with tree branches or other objects.

Brown Bear: Grizzly

xoóts in Lingit • Ursus arctos horribilis

Brennen Grizzly Bear reporting in. I'm the smaller of Alaska's brown bears, and I live in the interior areas of this great state. I may be smaller, but I'm as fierce and scrappy as any brown bear anywhere! I have to be because, for one thing, living on the treeless inland tundra provides no place to hide from danger. When another bear wants to fight for territory, or a hungry wolf pack slinks up to surround me, I can't just run to a tree and climb to safety like Beatrice Black Bear does. And for another thing, even if I did live near the woods, I'm just not built for climbing. My curved front claws are sharp hooks and four inches long! They would get stuck in the tree's trunk, or just be in the way of a good grip. In addition to that, I have a large, heavy hump of muscles on my back between my shoulders, which makes climbing difficult.

This hump does aid me in hunting down a critter for lunch, though. The muscles help me push off quickly and strongly when I sprint after a marmot, squirrel, or moose calf. Almost instantly, I run at speeds close to thirty-five miles per hour! And when I do grab my prey, my long claws trap them for good. Now, if a rodent does manage to dive back into its underground den, my hump muscles and long claws help me dig right into their home. This way, I don't miss a meal.

Speaking of food and appetites, you may have heard that I will make a meal out of you. Read on if you want to keep that from happening! I would rather not bother with you, but if I have the carcass of a caribou calf or some other food, don't get close. I don't share! Know, too, that our sows are just as protective of their cubs as I am of my food. You do not want to go anywhere near those mommas.

Finally, remember that grizzlies hibernate during the long, cold winter, sometimes as long as seven months. When I wake up and come out of my den in the spring, stay out of my way. I'm very hungry and not friendly. Greet me from far away, or better yet, do not greet me at all. Just stay far away, and LEAVE ME ALONE!

My Facts

SIZE:
Boar: body, 6–7 feet long, 3.5–4.5 feet tall at shoulder; weight, 300–500 pounds at the end of summer, 30 percent less at end of winter
Sow: 25 percent smaller than boar

COLOR:
Body: pale yellowish to dark brown
Hair on back: white-tipped, giving grizzled or frosted look

FOOD:
Omnivorous (about 80 percent vegetation, 20 percent meat): nuts, berries and other fruits, grasses, small mammals, any edible material

DANGERS:
Other bears, wolves, humans

YEARS I LIVE:
20–25 years, sow longer than boar

I live in inland, highlighted areas only.

Did You See Me? Tell Your Story! ______________________

____

____

____

DID YOU KNOW? A great place to see me is in Denali National Park. Ride to Wonder Lake on one of the camper buses, and look for me on the hillsides and in the dry riverbeds. I might even walk up to the bus on the road!

Beaver

paluqtaq in Alutiiq • Castor canadensis

TIMBERRR! Oh, hi. I'm Bernice Beaver, busy this autumn night. I just gnawed through the trunk of this tree, and now I will chew off some branches to patch the hole in our dam. Bucky, my partner for life, is underwater pushing stones and mud into the hole to help glue my branches in place. We must make our repairs quickly, so we don't lose water from the pond that was created behind the dam. That's our pond, where we built our lodge, our home!

The lodge is made with the same materials used for the dam, and this home is oh-so-cozy inside! It's about twelve feet across and three feet high, with two rooms. We dry off in the first room after swimming indoors through the underwater entrance, which is two or three feet below the pond's surface. The second room is larger, four or five feet across. We spend most of our time relaxing, sleeping, and eating in this room. Both rooms have above-water ledges padded with grass and leaves that keep us dry and warm. During the winter, the thick walls freeze as hard as rock, acting like insulation to keep us even toastier in the cold weather.

Now, if you notice, we built our lodge toward the center of the pond. We did this so our enemies have to swim if they want to catch us. And if a creature does invade our pond while we are collecting food or working on the lodge or dam, one of us will whack our long, wide tail on the water to warn everyone else. We dive immediately, then use our large, webbed hind feet and tail rudder to race inside our lodge. If we can't get to safety right away and have to hide, we can stay underwater as long as fifteen minutes. We have valves in our ears and nose that close to keep water out. Our eyes are protected by special coverings, or membranes, that let us see clearly through the pond water. As you might guess, with all these special adaptations (a-dap-TA-shuns) for being in the water, that is where we are the most comfortable and safest. On land, we are clumsy, and become easy prey for enemies, so you probably won't see us walking around.

WHACK! Oh, no! Bucky just slapped his tail on the water! Danger! I'm diving, so you better go hide, too!

My Facts

SIZE:
Male: body, up to 38 inches long; tail, 10 inches long, 6 inches wide; weight, 40–70 pounds
Female: often larger than male; both continue growing throughout lifespan

COLOR:
Body: glossy chestnut brown fur with dark, long outer guard hairs
Underfur: lighter brown
Tail: black

FOOD:
Herbivorous: on land, bark and first layer of trees, shrubs, leaves, and plants (not wood); in water, roots, stems, and leaves of aquatic plants

DANGERS:
Coyotes, wolves, bears, lynxes, wolverines, dogs, humans

YEARS I LIVE:
10–12 years

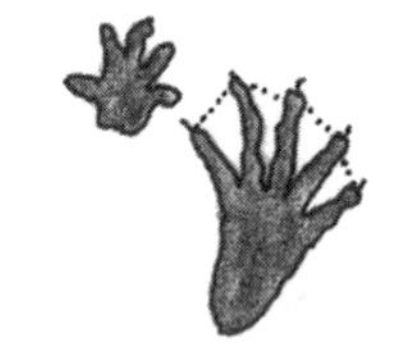

Did You See Me? Tell Your Story! ______________________________

____

____

____

DID YOU KNOW? Sometimes we build dens for homes in the banks of slow-moving rivers, lakes, or streams. Dens are made of the same materials as lodges. You will see a den on the bank of Jerome Lake on the road to Seward.

Plains Bison

xaas in Tlingit • Bison bison

My name is Brinkley Bison. I am the largest terrestrial (ter-REST-tree-ul), or land mammal, on the North American continent. This is the only continent on which I live, and no, I'm *not* a buffalo. I hear, "Oh, see that big buffalo over there?" all the time. I want to yell back, "No buffalo here! They all live in Africa and Asia." Since we are both in the bovine (BO-vine) family, though, and have some similarities, people who came here from Asia long ago started calling me "buffalo." But I'm different! My head is enormous, covered with thick hair, dropping to a distinguished goatee below my chin. My short horns grow out the sides of my head then curve straight up. (Our cows grow horns, too.) My body is massive and powerful, with a noticeable hump above my shoulders, a broad chest, and long, thick, shaggy hair that hangs down over my shoulders and front legs. And check out the way my back angles from my shoulder hump down to my narrow hindquarters, or rear end. This isn't how a buffalo is built. They look like a small cow, with short hair all over, a small head, and huge, long, curved pointed horns. They are little, while I'm a big, strong beast, more dangerous than Brennen Grizzly, but not as bad as his cousin, Brayden Brown Bear.

Nowadays, though, there aren't nearly as many of us bison as there are bears. When wooly mammoths lived long ago, there were millions of us! Then, during the last Ice Age, we roamed south to the Lower 48, where we were still the largest animal community anywhere. But, in the 1800s, hunters killed most of us for our meat or hides. A few hundred of us survived, though, and now we are rebuilding our herds. In 1928, twenty of us came home to Alaska, and currently, about nine hundred of us live here in four different herds. I stay with my gang near the Chitina River, and we travel around slowly, grazing and searching for food.

When I need to protect myself or chase off an intruder, I gallop a long way, moving as fast as thirty-five miles per hour. And you should know, I can be very unpredictable and savage. I attack with very little warning, so if I lower my head, snort, and paw the ground, with my tail raised upward, get away! This means I'm ready to charge. You need to be smart, and HIDE as fast as you can!

My Facts

SIZE:
Bull: body, 10 feet long, 6 feet tall at shoulder; weight, 2,000 pounds
Cow: body, 8 feet long, 5 feet tall at shoulder; weight, 1,200 pounds

COLOR:
Body: rich, dark brown in winter; lighter brown in spring and summer

FOOD:
Herbivorous: grasses, sedges, forbs, and leaves of vetch, silverberry, willow, birch, other trees and shrubs

DANGERS:
Wolves, big brown bears

YEARS I LIVE:
10–20 years or more

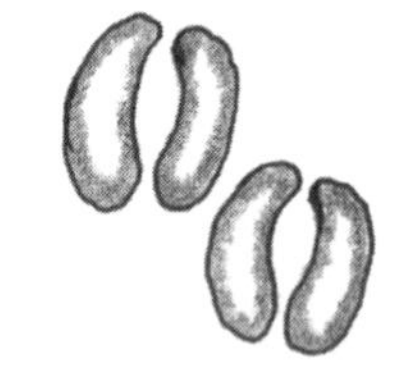

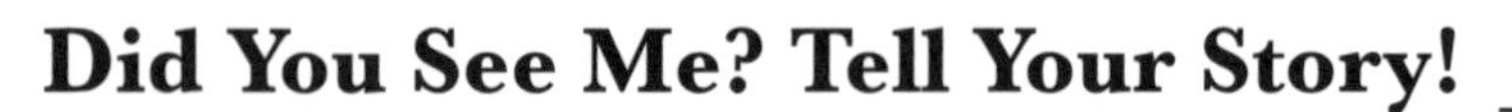

DID YOU KNOW? Herds of wood bison, my close relatives, were reintroduced in three areas of Alaska during the summer of 2015. These herds were raised in the Alaska Wildlife Conservation Center near the Portage turnoff. This is very exciting for us all!

Barren Ground Caribou

tutu in Inupiat • Rangifer tarandus granti

Hello! I'm Cordelia Caribou (CARE-a-boo), proud member of the deer family. Don't you love my beautiful, light brown antlers? I'm the only female, or doe, in the deer family who is able to grow antlers. They aren't very big or thick, growing only about a foot and a half tall, and they have only a few, small branches. But I think they are wonderful. Our bucks, though, *they* have huge sets of antlers! Theirs grow up to three feet across and four feet tall, filled with branches, points, and curved areas called "shovels." Magnificent! Bucks drop these antlers in October, but I keep mine until I give birth to my calf in May or June. Callie over there already had her baby, so her antlers just fell off. My calf will be here soon, and then my antlers will drop, too.

Speaking of calves, many of our babies are killed when they are first born. Bears, wolves, and human hunters are all so dangerous! We travel in huge herds of thousands upon thousands, but we still cannot protect all of the babies since so many are born at the same time. The ones who do survive have to keep up right away. They walk with the herd almost immediately, and within a week or so, they run and swim with us.

Swimming is so easy for me. You see, I have hollow hair cells that trap air to help me float high out of the water. Then my five-inch wide hooves, the roundest and widest of any in the deer family, act like big paddles to help push me through the water. I move really fast! These hooves help me on the terrain I travel, too. They keep me from sinking into soggy coastal areas, inland tundra, as well as the deep snow high in the mountains. You see, we journey up to nine hundred miles every year over all types of land, moving from our winter range to our spring calving grounds, and then on to our summer feeding areas. There are so many of us that if we didn't move, we would run out of food. So we roam all over this wonderful state, known as the nomads of the north. Now, if you see us, look carefully to find me. It may be difficult to pick me out of the herd, so yell and wave. I'll be on the lookout for you!

My Facts

SIZE:
Buck: body, 6–7 feet long, 3.5–4 feet tall at shoulder; weight, 250–400 pounds
Doe: body, 5-6 feet long, 3.5 feet tall at shoulder; weight, 175–225 pounds

COLOR:
Back: rich, clove brown
Neck, rump, side stripe: tan/white
Underside: light cream

FOOD:
Herbivorous: leaves, sedges, flowering plants, and mushrooms in summer; lichen, dried sedges, small shrubs in winter

DANGERS:
Wolves, bears, humans

YEARS I LIVE:
10–12 years

Did You See Me? Tell Your Story! ________________

____

____

____

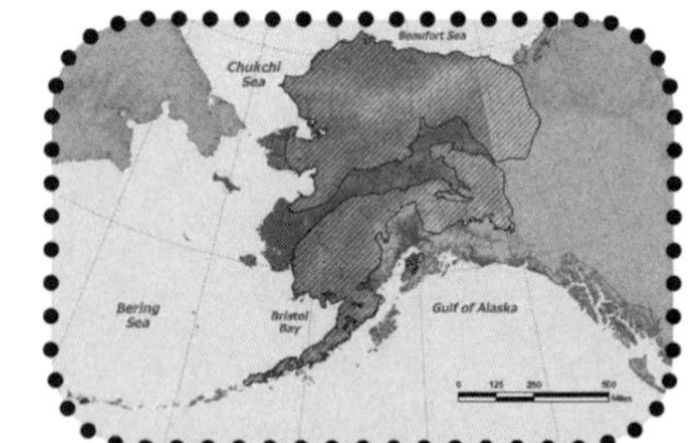

DID YOU KNOW? If we are raised on ranches in Alaska, we are called reindeer. Does that mean wild caribou and reindeer are the same animal? Do some research with a parent or teacher's help and find out what scientists say.

Coyote

xa in Haida • Canis latrans

Yo! Craig Coyote's the name. My Latin name, *Canis latrans*, means "barking dog," and man, do I love to make noise. When I'm just hanging out, I make little barks and growls. At night, though, you can hear my whole pack hunting. Listen for our short, high yips, followed by long, piercing howls, and finally some quick, noisy yaps.

So, did you ever wonder if you were hearing old Worthington Wolf instead of me? We are both part of the dog family and look alike, but I'm the noisier one, even though I'm smaller. I'm about one-third Mr. Wolf's size, shorter and thinner, with long, slender legs. My nose is longer, too, and very narrow and pointed. For my size, I have large ears, also pointed, and they always stand straight up. Worthington's nose and ears are smaller and rounded, and overall, he is stockier and larger than I am. The best way to tell us apart, though, is when we are running. A wolf's tail is high up in the air when he's cruising, and I keep my bushy tail down between my hind legs.

Ya' know, I'm just a running fool! I move smoothly and quickly anywhere from twenty-five to forty miles per hour, and I roam as much as one hundred miles when I'm looking for food. And speaking of food, I'm not choosey. I'm a scavenger (SCA-ven-jer), so I eat anything I find.

I especially love rodents, and when I spot one, I'm totally sneaky. I stretch way up on the tips of my toes to ease soundlessly toward the critter. Then, when I am as close as I can possibly be, I leap up in the air and pounce, landing right on top of my prey. Dinner!

I don't always hunt alone, either. My pack-mates and I hunt together to take down a bigger victim, like an elk or a caribou. One of us will jive and groove and make all kinds of sounds to get our prey's attention, while the rest of us move slowly to surround it. Then, all together, we attack! And we are good! We go for the throat, chomp down, and bring that big critter down. When we have had our fill, we cache, or save, the leftovers for later. So, if you see me, give a holler. If I feel like it, I might do a special howl back at you! Yeeeooowww!

My Facts

SIZE:
Body: 28–31 inches long, 21–24 inches tall at shoulders; tail, 11–16 inches; weight, 20–50 pounds

COLOR:
Body: grizzled black to light tan
Legs and muzzle: rusty
Tail: gray or black top with lighter underside; black tip

FOOD:
Omnivorous scavenger: rodents, eggs, carrion, hares, fish, berries

DANGERS:
Wolves, grizzlies, golden eagles, humans

YEARS I LIVE:
Up to 14 years

Did You See Me? Tell Your Story! ______________________________

____

____

____

DID YOU KNOW? I am larger than a fox and smaller than a wolf. Like both of them, I usually build my den in the ground. When I can, I steal someone else's old home so I don't have to start from scratch. Worthington Wolf's old den is perfect!

Sitka Black-Tailed Deer

Wun in Sm'algyax • Odocoileus hemionus sitkensis

Oh, hello. I'm Dottie Deer, smallest of the black-tailed deer. Welcome to my home in the coastal rainforest, where I'm staying with my twins, Dori and Dougie. They were born in late May, and because they are just a few weeks old, they need to grow bigger before we travel to the high, alpine meadow where I normally spend the summer. There are so many delicious plants and leaves up there! It's safer for them down here, though, because the forest provides much more protection than the open meadow. See their reddish-brown fur? That helps them blend right into the trees and undergrowth. And those clean, white spots on their backs look like the bright spots of light that speckle the forest floor on a sunny day. When Dougie and Dori curl up on the ground and are completely still, our enemies don't see them at all!

Soon, though, their spots will fade away, and my little fawns will grow up to look just like me: small, short, and stocky, with a short face and long ears. Oh, and Dougie? Each year, he will grow small, dark-brown antlers with three points on each side. Dori and I don't do antlers. That's a guy thing!

Eating isn't just a guy thing, though. We all have appetites to feed! And the food here in the forest isn't always easy to find, especially during a snowy winter. I prefer old-growth, thick forests where big trees block the snow from falling to the ground and covering up the food. Trees in young forests are farther apart and smaller, so more snow falls through making it difficult to find my berry bushes and other woody shrubs. If I do get stuck in a young forest, I often have to go out onto the beach at low tide to search for kelp and beach grass. Beach plants do not have the vitamins and minerals I need to stay strong and healthy, however, so I become dangerously thin on that diet. Even going out on the beach can mean big trouble. There is no place to hide from human hunters out there, and more than twelve thousand of my kind are killed every year by these hunters. They want us more than any other critter! That is why I am amazingly good at hiding. So, if you want to find me, you will have to look very carefully!

My Facts

SIZE:
Buck: body, 5–6 feet long, 3.5 feet tall at shoulders; weight, 120 pounds
Doe: 20 percent smaller than buck

COLOR:
Body: reddish-brown in summer; grayish-brown in winter
Tail: black on top year-round

FOOD:
Herbivorous: plants and green leaves, beach plants, berry trailings, woody browse

DANGERS:
Wolves, bears, coyotes, humans, hard winters

YEARS I LIVE:
6–12 years

Did You See Me? Tell Your Story! ____________________

____

____

____

DID YOU KNOW? Some of my favorite foods have interesting names: skunk cabbage, goose tongue, leaves of blue- and blackberries, marsh marigold, ground dogwood, salmonberry trailings, and my favorite, deer cabbage.

North American Elk

Cirunertulik in Sugpiaq • Cervus elaphus

Surprised to see me in this book? I'm Eric Elk, proud member of the deer family. I am much larger than Dottie Deer and Cordelia Caribou, but smaller than Mortimer Moose. Now, some people say there are no elk in Alaska. Wrong! We are here . . . again. You see, millions of years ago, during the Pleistocene (PLY-ste-Sene) epoch, my distant relatives lived throughout interior Alaska. The last ice age made it too cold to stay here, though, and everyone disappeared. Well, about one hundred years ago, we were reintroduced to Alaska, meaning we were brought back here from somewhere else. Eight Roosevelt elk calves were moved from the state of Washington to Algonak (al-GON-nak) and Raspberry Islands, north of Kodiak Island. At least nine hundred live there now. That's not all! In 1987, a herd of fifty Roosevelt and Rocky Mountain elk were transported from the state of Oregon to Etolin (et-TOE-lin) Island in Southeast Alaska. That herd is now over thirteen hundred, including some who swam to nearby islands or to the mainland.

In fact, one summer I swam to the mainland and climbed to the high, alpine mountain slopes where there are thick, spruce forests and vast, open meadows. Now, I hang out there every summer with a herd of at least twenty-five others. The plants and grasses are delicious in the meadows, and the forests provide places to hide from danger. And, while I am there every summer, I grow a set of massive, spreading antlers that sweep back over my shoulders. On the end of each branch are two or three sharp, pointed spikes which look like crowns. As my antlers grow, all the crowns, spikes, and branches are covered with soft velvet that protects them until they harden in the fall. When they are fully grown and solid, I rub the velvet off on tree trunks and low limbs. Then, in the winter, when I go down to the lower valleys to get away from the deep snow in the high meadow, I drop or lose my incredible antlers. All that beauty, gone, but I know I will grow new, even bigger antlers next summer. So, try to come see me in late summer, in the early morning or evening when I'm most active. If you do see me, wave and yell, "Hi, Eric!" Maybe I'll bugle back at you!

My Facts

SIZE:
Bull: body, 6–10 feet long, 4–5 feet tall at shoulder; weight, up to 1,300 pounds
Cow: 25 percent smaller than bull

COLOR:
Body: reddish-brown
Legs, belly, neck, head: dark brown
Rump: light yellow/tan patch
Tail: white

FOOD:
Herbivorous: grasses, sedges, fireweed, mushrooms, other plants in summer; woody plants, berry bushes, roots in winter

DANGERS:
Brown bears, humans, diseases, hard winters

YEARS I LIVE:
12–15 years

Did You See Me? Tell Your Story! ____________________

____

____

____

DID YOU KNOW? I have a very loud voice! At night I bugle a high-pitched whistle. Cows make a similar squeal, and bark loudly when the herd is traveling. The calves squeal when they are afraid. We are all very vocal critters!

Ermine or Short-Tailed Weasel

nihmaay in Tanacross • Mustela erminea

Emma Ermine is my name. Do I look gentle and sweet with all my beautiful fur? Well, I'm not. Actually, I'm quite ferocious (fur-O-shus). You see, I am bigger than my cousins in the Lower 48, and I am that much more threatening. If you look closely at my head, you will see how it is a little pointed in the front, then widens to a wedge shape, just like the deadly rattlesnake. That head, on this very slim, long body, along with these short legs, make it so easy for me to invade any tunnel, den, or burrow where my prey is hiding. If my head fits, I'm in like a snake, racing quickly after my victim.

And my jaw muscles? Whoa! They are very large and extremely strong. I can hold on to anyone's neck once I bite down. I use my front feet to grab my prey, and then I scratch and claw it to death with my hind feet. It's not pretty!

You should know, too, that when I'm on the hunt for a vole, woodchuck, or anyone else that looks like dinner, I am bold and curious. I dart one way, then I dash another, always looking and checking out anything that moves. Is it a meal? You see, I have to eat constantly because this long body makes is hard for me to stay warm in cold Alaska. Food helps me stay warm, but I have to eat one third to one half of my own body weight *every single day*! This means I have to consume three to four ounces of meat. So, if I catch Petie Pika and eat him, he's big enough to satisfy me for one day. But if I have to go after little Vinnie Vole and his kind, I need to catch three or four of them to fill my belly.

Once in a while I'm lucky enough to kill more food than I can eat, so I drag the carcass to my den where I cache, or save, it for later. This den is in a hollow log, or the stump and roots of an old tree near water. Looking for me near water is a good idea, but if you want to see me, you must be alert. I don't stand still for more than a second, and I probably won't wave. That wastes my time and energy. Try to find me!

My Facts

SIZE:
Buck: body, 12–14 inches long; tail, 4 inches long; weight, 6–8 ounces
Doe: 40 percent smaller than buck

COLOR:
Summer: back, rich brown; belly and feet, creamy white; tail, black-tipped
Winter: body, all white; tail, black-tipped

FOOD:
Carnivorous: small fish, voles, mice, other small mammals, insects

DANGERS:
Coyotes, mink, foxes, martens, raptors, humans and their traps

YEARS I LIVE:
1–2 years

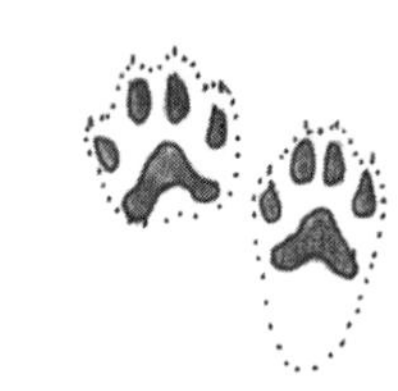

Did You See Me? Tell Your Story!

DID YOU KNOW? Every winter, my pelt, or fur, turns snow white except for the black tip on my tail. It is very dense and soft, making a wonderful winter coat. Humans set traps for me because they want to use my fur to make coats for themselves.

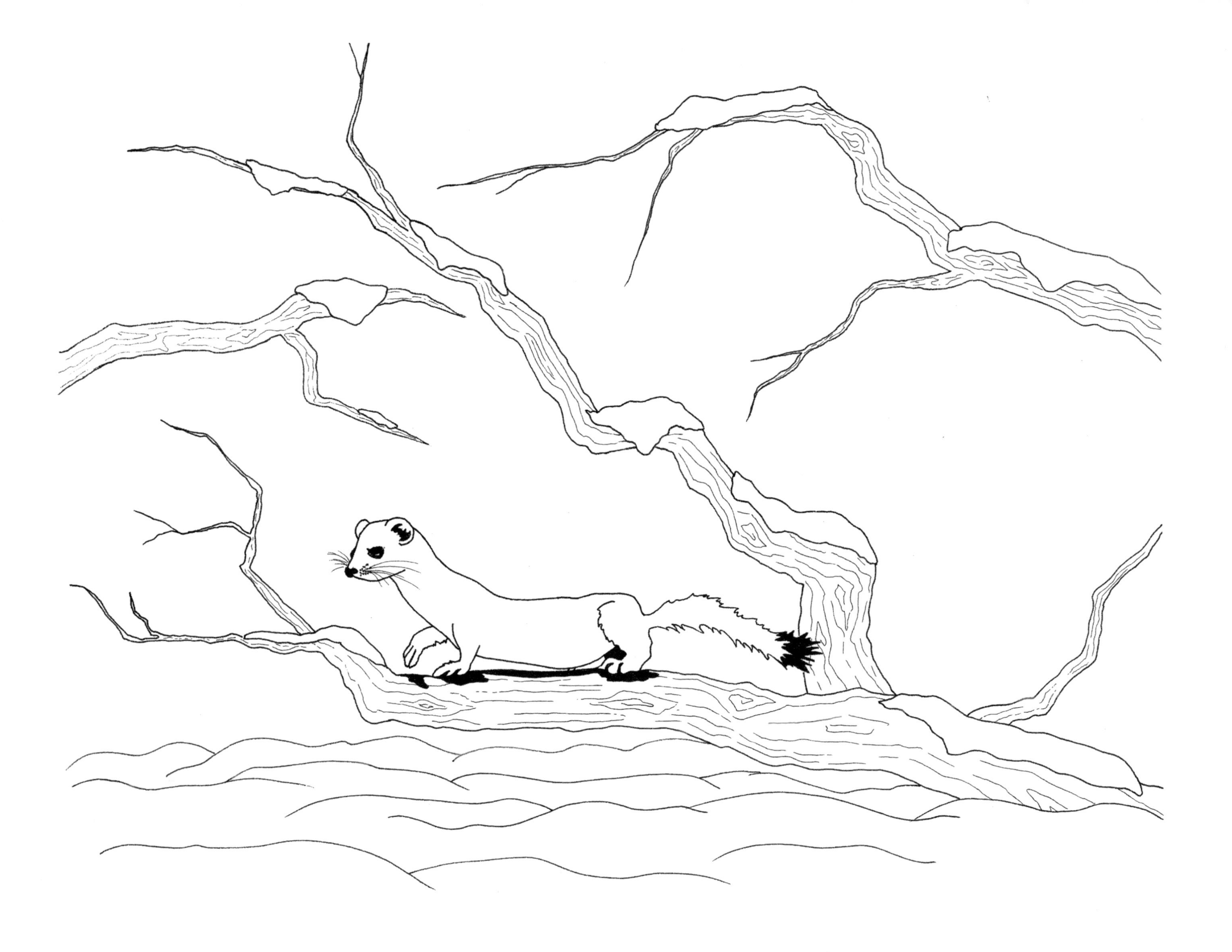

Arctic Fox

qaterlir in Yupik • Alopex lagopus

It's summertime! I'm Florence Fox, enjoying the sunshine outside my den. I built it under this log, in the sandy, well-drained slope of the riverbank. My den goes back into the bank, then it angles downward into the ground another ten feet. I use the same den every spring when I have my kits, or young, as it is so difficult to build a new den. You see, below the surface of the ground is permafrost, or permanently frozen earth, and digging through it is almost impossible.

Speaking of kits, these two are ready to face the day. My other four are resting inside right now, unless one of them wandered out another entrance. We have several entrances (or exits) in the den, to be sure there are plenty of ways to get in and out if an enemy comes too close. And right now, I'm on "kit duty" since my mate, Fred, is out hunting. We take turns providing food for the family until September or October, when the kits have grown big enough to hunt on their own. That's when we all go our separate ways until next spring, when Fred and I meet again, right here at our den, to have another family.

While I'm on my own, I might stay along the treeless, coastal areas or roam up onto the tundra. Most of the time, though, I'm on the shifting pack ice where I follow Bella Polar Bear and scavenge (SCAV-enj) behind her. I eat the leftover seals and other marine mammals she kills but doesn't finish eating. Bella doesn't wander as far as I do, however, so I won't trail her for long. I'm a wanderer, and I travel farther than any other land mammal, especially out on the ice.

And no, I don't get cold on the frozen ground. My feet are thickly furred, and my chubby body is very compact, with short legs and muzzle, and small rounded ears. I have very little surface area exposed to the cold air. Also, my white winter coat, with long, thick, hollow fur, traps air, which my body warms. I stay comfortable even when the temperatures drop to minus seventy degrees. But now, it's summertime and so much warmer. I am wearing my grayish-brown topcoat, which isn't nearly as thick nor as warm as my winter one.

Oh, darn! I hear kits fighting inside. I'd better check on them. Wave from a distance if you find our den!

My Facts

SIZE:
Body: 18–26 inches long, 9-12 inches tall at shoulder; tail, 11–14 inches long; weight, 8–12 pounds

COLOR:
White phase: winter, all white;
Summer, brown-gray upper with light belly
Blue phase: blue-gray all year

FOOD:
Omnivorous scavenger: voles, lemmings, rodents, hares, sea birds, eggs, berries, carrion

DANGERS:
Wolves, polar bears, owls, golden eagles, humans

YEARS I LIVE:
5–10 years

Did You See Me? Tell Your Story! ______________________

____

____

____

DID YOU KNOW? My keen hearing allows me to hear small critters tunneling through the snow in the wintertime. To catch them, I leap high in the air, and then land hard enough to break through the snow and trap them. An easy meal!

Red Fox

nagats'ee in Sm'algyax • Vulpes vulpes

Hey! I'm Farley, one very cool, Old World red fox who looks like a hip, red dog. Most of my clan are a rich, reddish-yellow color with black legs and feet. We have incredibly bushy tails that are a mixture of long, red and black fur. A few of us, though, are black with white-tipped fur, while still others have a dark cross over their shoulders and down their backs. It can be confusing, so just remember that we all have a white chest and belly that matches the white tip on our bushy tails.

Now, I hear there are rumors going around about me. Did I really escape three traps last week? You bet I did. I'm curious, intelligent, cunning, and definitely difficult to catch. I check out interesting-looking contraptions, but I'm cautious and stay clear of danger.

I hear there's another rumor about me being paranoid, or totally suspicious of everyone and everything. Maybe I am. I know that I like this open country where I can see enemies from a long way off, and I love the forest where I hide from critters who scare me. But you also might find me in lowland marshes or running through the rolling hills on the tundra. I trot all over the place, usually at about five miles per hour. In the winter, though, I travel great distances looking for food. That's when I speed up to twenty miles per hour.

I'm usually on my own, except when there are pups to be raised. I'm a great dad, working hard to share responsibilities with my vixen, or mate. I find a den for the family, even if I have to chase a critter out of its own place. I prefer using Worthington Wolf's empty den because I don't have to enlarge it. I share feeding responsibilities, too. Either my mate or I stay at the den with the pups while the other goes hunting. When I spot a tasty varmint, I sneak up silently, leap way up in the air, and pounce straight down to trap the critter in my claws. Easy! I keep our pups well-fed until they can hunt on their own, which happens when they are about six months old. That's when we say our good-byes, and split up to go it alone again. Right now, I'm scoping out my next meal. So I'm splitting to go my own way, and you go yours. Got it?

My Facts

SIZE:
Dog: body, 22–25 inches long; tail, 15 inches long; weight, 6–15 pounds
Vixen: usually weighs less than dog

COLOR:
Body: usually reddish
Belly: white
Legs: black
Tail: bushy with white tip

FOOD:
Omnivorous: voles, mice, hares, squirrels, muskrats, carrion, birds, eggs, berries, vegetation

DANGERS:
Wolves, coyotes, lynxes, wolverines, bears, humans, golden eagles (pups)

YEARS I LIVE:
3–10 years

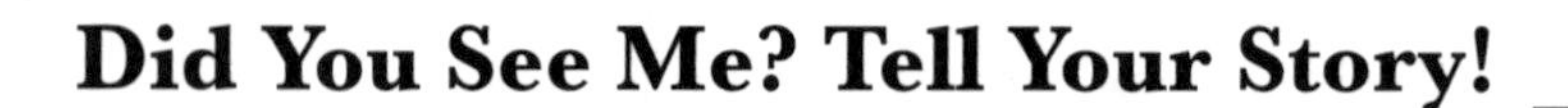

Did You See Me? Tell Your Story! ______________________

____

____

____

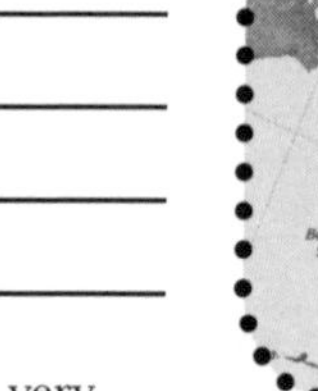

DID YOU KNOW? Sometimes I roam into the far north where my cousin Florence Arctic Fox lives. When I do, I'm not very kind to her. In fact, I have been known to chase her into her den, then dig her out and kill her. I don't know why I do it, but I do.

Mountain Goat

ja ẖwu in Lingit • *Oreamnos americanus*

Man! Sure is windy up here on these steep, coastal mountains! I'm Gregory-James Goat, the only rock goat in North America. I love it on the extremely high, sheer slopes of these craggy, old mountains. Even trees don't grow where I live! And it gets freezing cold in the winter, so every year I grow this long, shaggy, heavy coat to stay warm. I'm covered with coarse, guard hairs that are at least seven inches long, giving me this fluffy, puffy look. Around my neck, the mane of hair gives me what looks like a beard, too. Now, I need all this hair in the winter, but in the summer it's too hot, so I shed most of these long outer hairs and stay warm with a much thinner coat. That's when you see that I am actually very sleek and slim with a compact, muscular body.

My body shape, along with the incredible strength I have in my front quarters and shoulders, allows me to walk and jump quickly and safely on the cliffs and narrow ledges. It's like being on tightropes all the time, so I need this thin, flat-sided build to hug the rocks and keep from falling to my death. My short legs help with my balance on the ledges, too, as do my hooves that are specially adapted for this terrain. They are hard keratin (KARE-a-tin) on the outside, but on the bottom, they are rough like sandpaper and rubbery soft. The soft part gives me ultimate gripping power on the rocks, then spreads out to act like brakes when I need to keep from sliding. I may not be able to outrun my enemies, but I move easily along terrain where no predator dares to go. Avalanches and rockslides are much more dangerous for me than any beast!

And please, don't confuse me with Sheila Dall Sheep. She lives in mountains, too, but usually down at lower elevations. We're both white, but I'm more yellowish. Remember about my thin sides? Well, Sheila is much chubbier than I am, with a full, round belly. Also, my short, black horns stick straight up with a slight backward curve, and look like slender daggers. Her horns are thick, golden-colored, and make a downward curl. And the horns on their rams are even bigger and make absolutely huge curls! So look closely to be sure it's me, and then wave big so I see you!

My Facts

SIZE:
Billy: body, 4–6 feet long, 3–3.5 feet tall at shoulder; weight, 100–300 pounds
Nanny: 40 percent smaller than billy

COLOR:
Body: white to yellowish-white
Eyes, nose, hooves, horns: black

FOOD:
Herbivorous: grasses, herbs, shrubs, twigs and leaves of hemlock trees, mosses, lichen, blueberries

DANGERS:
Wolves, brown bears, humans, avalanches, rockslides

YEARS I LIVE:
12–18 years

Did You See Me? Tell Your Story! ____________________

____

____

____

DID YOU KNOW? People love watching us jump along the jagged cliffs. Usually our herd is eight to twelve, but sometimes forty or fifty of us gather. Too many together, though, often leads to someone falling. An accident? Maybe.

Snowshoe Hare

kushaanaq in Sugpiaq • Lepus americanus

Hi, I'm Helga Snowshoe Hare, and we have to LOOK OUT! I think Lloyd Lynx is lurking behind those snow-laden spruce trees! If he is, you will see me leap and twist and dodge so he doesn't catch me. If he does start chasing me, I might even have to do some boxing to survive! You see, I'm just about all Lloyd and those dangerous lynxes eat. And, because I don't hibernate in the winter, I have to be on the lookout for him all the time!

It helps that my eyes protrude (pro-TROOD), or stick out from my head a little bit. This gives me almost three hundred and sixty-degree vision to watch in all directions. My tall ears each swivel or turn on their own, too, so I can hear Lloyd trying to ambush me from any direction. Did you notice my huge, furry hind feet? Big thumpers, aren't they? They are about five inches long, giving me amazing traction, leverage, and speed when I am running on the snow. It's like having built-in snowshoes. In fact, that's where I got my name.

But even with all this, Lloyd finds plenty of us to eat. He is fast and cunning, so it's a good thing I have so many babies, or leverets (lev-er-RETs), in the summer months. I usually have two or three litters, with at least four leverets in each litter. But only one or two of my babies will survive as long as two weeks, and just a few of those make it to a year. Sophie Red Squirrel and her family are the worst ones for terrorizing my nest, or form, as I call it. Even when I stomp my feet, click my teeth, make a horrible racket, and act crazy, those squirrels get past me and attack my nest. It's awful!

It's strange, too, how my kind goes through "boom or bust" population cycles every ten years or so. That means, when there is plenty of food, we have more leverets and more of them survive. With so many of us, however, food is used up, so we have fewer babies, and fewer of them survive. And when there are fewer of us, there are fewer lynxes, too. Their population depends on ours.

Oh, no! I hear something. If I stand around talking anymore, Lloyd is going to have one more hare dinner. I'm so out of here . . . NOW!

My Facts

SIZE:
Body: 18–20 inches long; ears, 3.5–4 inches tall; weight, 2–4 pounds

COLOR:
Winter: white all over
Summer: back and sides, brownish-gray; belly, white
Eyes, nose, ear tips: black

FOOD:
Herbivorous: grasses, and the buds, twigs, leaves, bark, or needles from willow, birch, aspen, alder, and hemlock trees

DANGERS:
Lynxes, foxes, martens, coyotes, mink, hawks, owls, red squirrels (newborn leverets)

YEARS I LIVE:
2–4 years

Did You See Me? Tell Your Story! ______________________

____

____

____

DID YOU KNOW? There are no wild rabbits here in Alaska. It's a good thing, as their babies are born without hair or fur and their eyes are closed. My babies are born covered with fur with their eyes open, hopping around right away.

Tundra or Alaska Hare

maqaruar in Yupik • Lepus othus

Do you think I look big for a hare? Well, you're right! Hector Tundra Hare here, also known as the Alaska Hare. My massive head and huge body make me one of the largest hares in North America. Helga Snowshoe Hare looks miniature next to me.

Some people call me an Arctic hare . . . well, I'm not. We're close relatives, but our teeth and skulls are different. I'm the western branch of the family, with the others in northeastern Canada and up into Greenland. I live here, usually alone, near the Alaska shorelines in the dense alder thickets of the coastal tundra, or out on an alluvial (al-LOO-vee-al) plain. Or I might be in the sedge flats and wet meadows. Or I might even be on the open tundra, though I prefer the safety of brushy areas where it is easier to find places to hide.

No matter where I'm hanging out, I am one huge, hairy hare. When I stand up straight, I am two feet tall. Plus, I weigh up to twelve pounds, which is more than most pet cats weigh. I'm enormous! Oh, and my big, furry, hind feet measure about seven inches long. These huge paws help me move over the snow without falling through it. But you know what's weird? My ears are very short. They are only about three inches long, which is shorter than my head. This is a good thing, actually. Short ears don't lose as much heat as long ones, helping me stay warm in the cold, Alaska winters.

Speaking of winter, that's when I turn completely white, right down to my skin, except for the black tips of my ears. I hide easily in the snow. But it's summer now, so I've grown my colorful pelage (pe-LAJE), or fur. It is brownish with a touch of gray mixed in, making me look grizzled. My belly and tail stay white, though. And summer is when I must be especially careful to avoid the dangerous metal traps humans set for me. My fur is thick and soft, and your kind uses it for lining boots and making robes. Some even cook me up for dinner! Horrible! So I stay alert, and hide quickly if I see something on two legs. You'll have to look very carefully and be very quiet if you want to catch a glimpse of me!

My Facts

SIZE:
Body: 20–26 inches long; ears, 3.5 inches tall; weight, 10–12 pounds

COLOR:
Back and sides: winter, white; summer, grizzled or light brown
Nose, mouth, eyes: black

FOOD:
Herbivorous: willow bark and leaves, shrubs, leaves, buds, roots, grasses, crowberries, kelp, marine plants

DANGERS:
Hawks, eagles, falcons, owls, red foxes, wolves, weasels, polar bears, humans

YEARS I LIVE:
2–3 years

Did You See Me? Tell Your Story! ____________________

____

____

____

DID YOU KNOW? Our females have only one litter of five to seven leverets a year. This large litter is born soon after the snow disappears, and the newborns stay in the unlined form, or nest, much longer than snowshoe hare babies do.

Brown Lemming

pugultu in Yupik • *Lemmus trimucronatus*

If you see a stout, stubby-tailed, hairy-footed little rodent hiding in the bushes, it's probably me. Hi. I'm Lynna Lemming, the only true lemming in Alaska and the largest of lemmings anywhere! There are voles, mice, and shrews here, too, and we all look somewhat alike. Just remember: I'm the largest and roundest, have a very furry body with a hairless tail that looks like a pointed stump, and little ears that get lost in my loose fur. Vinnie Vole and I actually look the most alike, because we both have reddish backs and rumps, and yellowish-brown color everywhere else. He may change color to hide more easily, though, depending on where he lives. I'm just the same old color most of the time, maybe a little grayer in the summer. So it's probably easiest for you to remember that I'm round and chubby.

And now that you can recognize me, I need to set the record straight about something else. There have been rumors about lemmings for many years. People say we gather in big groups, run to the edges of high cliffs, and jump to our death. NO! We do NOT do that, ever! Nor do we migrate, or move from place to place. We stay in our own little territory and are active all year round. But something strange does happen to us. We have "wide population changes." What does that mean? Well, in some years, there are thousands and thousands of us. Then, within three to five years, nearly all of us are gone. It's like we disappear almost completely.

Why does this happen? No one knows for sure. It might be that when our population is high, there isn't enough food, so some of us starve. Maybe the many critters who think we're tasty become better at finding us under the little shrubs where we hide on the open tundra. (We are an important food source for many, so *shh*! Keep our hiding place a secret.) Another reason might be that, since we don't hibernate in the cold, cold winters, we freeze to death. After all, we do run around both day and night, and nights are so cold here! No one really knows for sure why we disappear, but I do know I am alive and kicking right now. Try to find me, and yell, "Hello!" if you do!

My Facts

SIZE:
Body: 4–5 inches long; tail, 0.5–1 inch short; weight, 2–4 ounces

COLOR:
Lower back and rump: reddish
Sides: brownish-yellow to pale buff

FOOD:
Herbivorous: grasses and sedges in summer; mosses, bark, and twigs in winter

DANGERS:
Weasels, arctic foxes, wolves, wolverines, predatory birds

YEARS I LIVE:
1–2 years

Did You See Me? Tell Your Story! ____________________

____

____

____

Chukchi Sea

Bering Sea

Bristol Bay

Gulf of Alaska

DID YOU KNOW? When our population is at its highest, you might see me in places I normally do not live. I move to the edges of the tundra and alpine meadows looking for food. I even go out on the sea ice to escape the crowds!

Canadian Lynx

Duusmgyilhawl: in Sm'algyax • Lynx canadensis

I meow, I purr . . . Am I a cat? Yup, you're right! I'm Lloyd Lynx, the only wild cat native to Alaska. You would know for sure I'm a feline, or cat, if you saw or heard the cubs of my kind. They look just like regular pet kittens, and they sound the same with their soft purring and meows. As a grown-up, though, I'm different from any cat you know. First of all, I sound like I'm screaming at you, not purring, when I "talk." And if you annoy me, I respond with a very deep, frightening, menacing warning sound that means, "Stay away!"

I have a unique body, too. I'm large and muscular, and quick on my long, strong legs. My tail is very short, like it was chopped off. My ears are tipped with black tufts that look like feathers. And under my chin, I have a distinct ruff, or fringe, of fur that hangs down. Now, take a look at my feet, and this is important! They are gigantic, covered with thick fur on top and bottom, and work like snowshoes to keep me from sinking into deep snow. This is critical, for when I hunt Helga Snowshoe Hare and her band, I have to be fast, especially since I hunt at night. I stalk her and sneak up very close, then pounce in one or two leaps to catch her. If I sink down in the snow, she's gone, and that's bad for me. You see, those hares are my mainstay, or the most important food in my diet.

Oh, I'll eat rodents or birds in a pinch, but during the winter when I am awake instead of hibernating like others, food is a serious problem. Birds I like to eat migrate south, and the tasty little rodents I enjoy go to sleep until spring. The young of bigger critters I savor aren't born until the weather warms. So who is here? Helga Snowshoe Hare.

Now, when the hare population is high, I eat well, feel great, and life is good. But every eight to ten years, those darn hares disappear almost completely from the face of the Earth. Then we lynxes decrease in number, too. I hate to say it, but my survival depends on hers. So I roam over the river and through the woods looking for that elusive hare. I go where the hares go. Want to join me?

My Facts

SIZE:
Male: body, 30–40 inches long, 24–28 inches tall at shoulder; tail, 3–5 inches long; weight, 13–30 pounds
Female: up to 40 percent smaller than male

COLOR:
Body: light tan with gray and black streaks, scattered black spots

FOOD:
Carnivorous: snowshoe hares (primarily), grouse, ptarmigan, mice, squirrels, salmon, baby foxes, sheep

DANGERS:
Wolves, wolverines, humans

YEARS I LIVE:
5–11 years

Did You See Me? Tell Your Story! ______________________________

____

____

____

DID YOU KNOW? I am a solitary creature who sleeps during the day and hunts at night. Sound like a typical cat? Well, I climb trees like a pet cat, but I bet your cat doesn't swim like I do! In the water, I'm fearless and fast.

Hoary Marmot

kuyxi in Ahtna • Marmota caligata

Tweeeeet! Brennen Grizzly Bear is in the area! HIDE!

Oh, hi. I'm Maya Marmot, the most common of the three marmots in Alaska, and I'm only going to visit with you for a minute. Danger is near! You heard my incredibly loud, shrill whistle? It carries for over a mile and warns everyone that a predator is close. In fact, my nickname is Whistler. Quite fitting, don't you think?

Even when there's no danger, I'm still a noisy rodent. You see, I'm the largest member of the squirrel family, and I talk and chatter constantly, using my large repertoire (REP-e-twar) of yips, whines, barks, hisses, and growls. It's important that I talk so much because everyone in our colony gets along extremely well, and we like to tell one another what's happening. But even though we all get along, we each have our own den, built into a talus slope, or rockslide, usually near a meadow in the mountains. My den is right below me in this big jumble of rocks at the bottom of this hillside. That's where I've been on lookout duty all day, watching for trouble.

The rocks protect me from enemies who try to dig me out of my den, and, if someone does start breaking into my home, I dive into the handy tunnel that leads to the underground maze connecting my den to all the other homes in the colony. I will be in Marge or Mabel's den within minutes if needed.

When the weather is warm during the daytime, and the pesky mosquitoes are out (they love marmot blood), we visit each other by using the underground routes to avoid being bitten by those nasty insects. We also avoid mosquitoes by going outside to eat and to play in the early morning or late afternoon or on breezy, overcast days. Mosquitoes don't like wind or cool temperatures, and I don't like cold either.

In fact, I stay in my den, sound asleep, from September until May. I am a real hibernator, (HI-ber-na-tor), meaning I go into a deep, deep sleep. I plug my den's entrance and opening to the tunnel; my heart rate becomes very slow; and my temperature goes way down. I don't wake up at all until it's warm and sunny outside.

Oh, no! I have to get going! Brennen's coming closer, and he is BIG trouble! Remember to listen for my whistle! *Twweeet!*

My Facts

SIZE:
Male: body, 18–22 inches long; tail, 7–10 inches long; weight, 10–20 pounds
Female: 20 percent smaller than male

COLOR:
Upper back: grizzled gray and white
Lower back, rump: light beige
Tail: brown top, dark under, light tip
Feet: black

FOOD:
Omnivorous: bird eggs, forbs, grasses, flowers, berries, roots, mosses

DANGERS:
Wolverines, wolves, bears, foxes, coyotes, golden eagles (kits)

YEARS I LIVE:
8–12 years

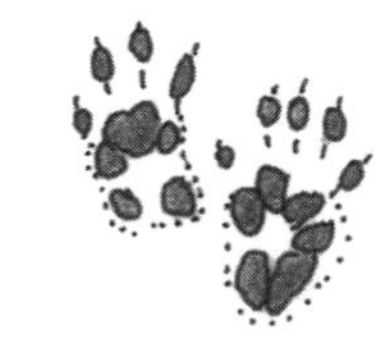

Did You See Me? Tell Your Story! ______________________

____

____

____

DID YOU KNOW? When I was young, I played a lot. Playtime included standing on my hind legs and pushing my friends around. It looked like we were fighting, but it was just for fun. Don't do this with your friends, though, so you don't get into trouble!

American Marten

k'uu in Haida • Martes americana

Hey! I'm Marley, a marten who knows what's going on! Did you know that I have another name? Well, I do. Some people call me the American sable, which tells you I have the most valuable, highly prized fur of any animal here in Alaska. My coat is incredibly soft, surprisingly long, and very dense, or thick, making it amazingly warm. My fur has made me the most widely hunted and trapped animal in Alaska. This is a serious problem, but I'm a fighter. They won't take me easily! Long, sharp claws help me be an agile, quick climber, and I'm up trees in a flash. In the winter, when there is snow, I tunnel under it as far as necessary to find safety. (I don't hibernate, so I'm awake all winter.) If all that fails, I simply turn around and fight, fight, fight to the death!

Of course, being hunted all the time is extremely stressful, and I am usually a nervous wreck. It's no wonder I dash around in such a frenzy, darting one way then another, through the coniferous (con-NIF-er-ous) and mixed-wood forests where I live. My den is in the forest, well-hidden in a hole in an old tree. And when I come out to hunt early in the morning or in the darkness at night, I zigzag in all directions, always staying near the forest. I may roam up to five miles away from my den to find food, but I never move far from the trees so that a safe hiding place is always easy to reach. If I make a kill out in the open, I immediately head for cover, taking my food with me. I do the same thing when I come across the remains of someone else's meal. I steal their carcass and drag it into the forest as fast as I can. You'd be amazed at the leftovers I steal with my natural curiosity and need to investigate everything!

Now, if you want to find me, look for a foxlike body with a short muzzle and face. My black eyes, whiskers, and nose cap are pretty obvious, and so are my broad, rounded ears that stand straight up. I'm the only one in the weasel family with a long, bushy tail and large, furry feet. So keep your eyes open. I'll be moving like a lightning bolt!

My Facts

SIZE:
Male: body, 19–25 inches long; tail, 6–9 inches long; weight, 2–4 pounds
Female: 30 percent smaller than male

COLOR:
Body: yellowish to dark brown; wide, orange-brown streak from throat to chest and inner legs
Tail and feet: black-tipped

FOOD:
Omnivorous: mice, voles, hares, insects, eggs, small birds, berries, vegetation, carrion

DANGERS:
Lynxes, red foxes, coyotes, raptors, owls, humans

YEARS I LIVE:
10–12 years

Did You See Me? Tell Your Story!

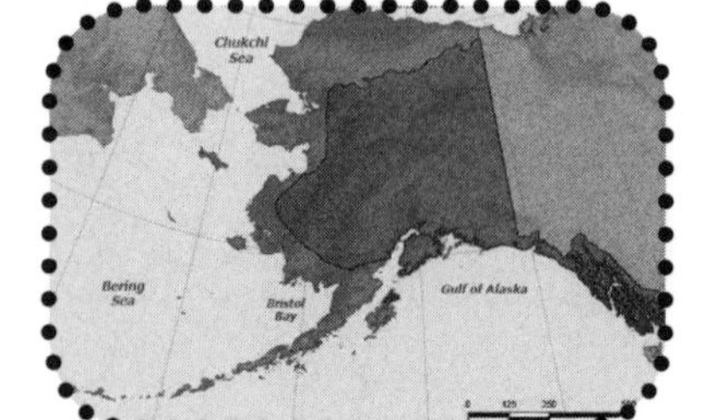

DID YOU KNOW? I belong to the same family as Madeline Mink, and we are similar in size and shape. My throat and chest are lighter than the rest of me, while she's the same color all over. Also, she likes water, and I like the trees.

American Mink

lukshiyaán in Lingit • Neovision vison

I just caught the best fish dinner! Hi, I'm Madeline Mink, fishing in one of my favorite spots. Most of my food comes from the water, and any aquatic (a-QUA-tic) critter I catch, I eat. I hunt mainly at night, roaming alone near marshes, ponds, and streams, and even out onto saltwater beaches. My route is usually the same, taking me at least five miles from my den, which is in a hollow tree or a stump near some kind of water. While I prefer to eat fish and other aquatic life, I do hunt for voles and other small mammals. They make easy snacks for an aggressive, fearless hunter like me. The fact is this: I am a dangerous eating machine with powerful jaws that easily crush any critter I catch!

The water is still my favorite place to be, though, and you should see me swim! I have a long, slim body, pointed nose, or muzzle, and small, compact head. It's the perfect body for swimming. And my short, strong legs and partially webbed toes help me zoom after my prey. I don't just swim on top of the water, either. When I want a fish swimming in a lake, or crustacean (crus-STAY-shun) on the bottom of a pond or tidal pool along the beach, I dive as deep as forty feet. I never become chilled in the icy waters of Alaska, since my thick, heavy outer fur has oily guard hairs that keep me completely dry and warm. My underfur, the fur closest to my body, is only an inch long but extremely thick and wavy. This coat insulates me, keeping me toasty warm.

My fur is a problem, though. It is a beautiful, rich, chocolate-brown color, as well as being soft and warm. Many people want their own mink coat, making me one of the most valuable fur-bearing animals in the world! Trappers and hunters are always trying to find me, but I'm good at dodging them. I'm hard to see at night, and I'm smart enough to stay well-hidden when I hear their heavy footsteps. I stay alert and avoid their traps. There are more of my kind now than there used to be, so I'm clearly doing a good job avoiding danger.

So be aware that you must stay alert if you want to see me. I will probably run away and hide if I see you first. Good luck finding me!

My Facts

SIZE:
Male: body, up to 17 inches long; tail, 9 inches long; weight, 3 pounds
Female: body, up to 14 inches long; tail, 7 inches long; weight, 2.5 pounds

COLOR:
Body: rich, chocolate brown
Chin, throat, and belly: white patches

FOOD:
Carnivorous: muskrats, fish, crab, clams, small mammals, anything caught

DANGERS:
Wolves, foxes, lynxes, river otters, owls, hawks, humans

YEARS I LIVE:
7–10 years

Did You See Me? Tell Your Story! ______________________

____

____

____

DID YOU KNOW? When I am afraid or very excited, I protect myself by spraying a strong, stinky liquid into the air, just like a skunk. The spray comes from the scent glands near my tail. And just so you know, there are no skunks in Alaska.

Moose

tunturpak in Sugpiaq • Alces alces

Greetings. I'm Mortimer Moose, Alaska's official state mammal and the largest member of the deer family. I'm the creature most people want to see when they visit Alaska, and I am certainly worth seeing. I am larger than most horses, with long, slender legs that look like stilts.

Look closely! You'll see I'm not level from front to back. I tilt downward from my shoulders to my rump, like a German Shepherd dog. Longer front legs are helpful when I need to jump logs, fences, or other obstacles, and also when I want to eat leaves or twigs high in a willow tree. But when I want to eat from the ground or from the bottom of a pond, my neck is too short for these front legs. I have to widen my stance in front to reach the ground. Sometimes I even have to kneel down like I'm praying if I want to eat!

Now, if you think that sounds odd, look at my nose. It is frightfully long with a huge, puffy, bulbous (BUL-bus) end. My nose is so elongated (e-LAWN-gated), it hangs down over my mouth! Unique, don't you think? I must say, though, my most uncommon body part is the long, thin patch of fur that hangs down under my chin. It is called a "bell" or "dewlap," and it looks like a long, skinny goatee. But my dewlap is softer than whiskers and swings from side to side as I move. Very dignified, in my opinion.

If you want to see my handsome figure, look for me in forested areas of willow and birch trees, especially near water. I eat twigs and leaves from the trees, and, in water, I devour the plants on the bottom of ponds, streams, and swamps. (I love to swim, incidentally.) But don't limit your search for me to the wilderness. I live in cities, towns, and villages, as well. I roam down streets and sidewalks, onto playgrounds, even into neighborhoods that are full of plants and blooming flowers. I am a road danger, also, because I cross highways and streets without looking both ways first.

I am large and in charge wherever I go, so you need to be careful. I will charge YOU if I'm annoyed. Be smart and read "Moose Safety" in this book, if you want to be safe around me. I'm a wild, unpredictable critter who likes his space.

My Facts

SIZE:
Bull: body, 8–10 feet long, 6–8 feet tall at shoulder; weight, up to 1,800 pounds
Cow: 25–40 percent smaller than bull

COLOR:
Body: varies from yellow to mixed browns and black
Legs: light-colored
Calves: born reddish-brown

FOOD:
Herbivorous: plants, leaves, grasses, water plants in summer; willow, aspen, and birch twigs in winter

DANGERS:
Wolves, bears, humans, vehicles

YEARS I LIVE:
15–20 years

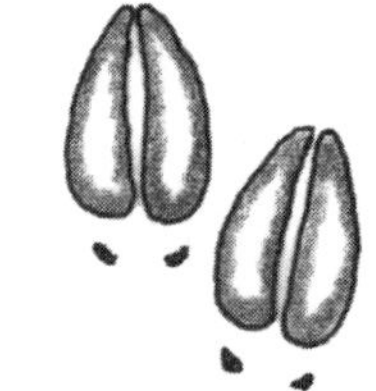

Did You See Me? Tell Your Story!

____

____

____

____

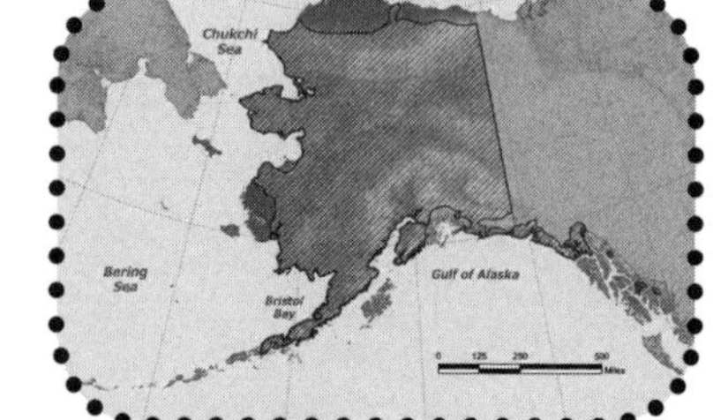

DID YOU KNOW? I'm a bull moose, so I grow massive antlers shaped like the palm of your hand with your fingers spread out. My antlers weigh as much as 80 pounds and may be up to eight feet across. Females, or does, do not grow antlers.

Muskox

xaas in Tlingit • Ovibos moschatus

Oh, I have such a horrible headache! But I'll tell you more about that later. I'm Murph Muskox, and I am one mighty, stocky, shaggy dude. As you see in my picture, my topcoat is extremely heavy with very long, coarse, outer hair. I am so shaggy my hair almost touches the ground! Can you tell I have a hump above my shoulders? I do, but it is very hard to see because of all this clumpy hair. But do you want to know my real secret? The hair underneath this mop, all over my body, up my nose, even between my toes, is worth a fortune! It is one of the rarest fibers in the whole world! It is totally smooth, amazingly soft, and incredibly warm. Alaska Natives call this hair *qiviut*, pronounced "KIV-e-oot." People in Alaska collect this hair and use it to create warm clothing. If you want to buy a scarf or gloves made from my *qiviut*, you will have to pay big bucks.

I have something else that is much more important and valuable to me, though. Know what? On the front of my head is my marvelous set of amber-colored horns. These are my pride and joy. See how they angle down, then swoop up in a very cool curve? And right in the center front of my forehead, I have at least four inches of horn growing on top of thick bone. (The cows have much thinner bone there than us bulls do!) This is my headgear, and it is so important to me because it protects my head when I am battling. We bulls like to show who is the toughest and the strongest, so we crash our heads together in great fights. We back way up, then run at each other and *wham*! We crash! It hurts like crazy, so having thick, strong headgear and horns is like wearing a helmet. In fact, I just battled with old Morton Muskox over there and showed him who's boss! My head hurts, but old Mort can hardly move. I'm the strongest of them all, but *shhh!* Please don't tell anybody I have this horrible headache.

And by the way, the best place to visit me is on my farm near Palmer. Otherwise, you will have to look for me in the remote areas of Alaska. I'm a long way from most cities. Do come visit, and maybe old Mort will agree to a rematch so you can see how we fight!

My Facts

SIZE:
Bull: body, 5–7 feet long, 4–5 feet tall at shoulder; weight, 500–1100 pounds
Cow: 20 percent smaller than bull

COLOR:
Body: shaggy, dark brown outer hair
Head, center back: lighter brown
Belly, undercoat, *qiviut:* light beige

FOOD:
Herbivorous: grasses, sedges, forbs, and other plants

DANGERS:
Wolves, polar bears, hunters

YEARS I LIVE:
12–18+ years

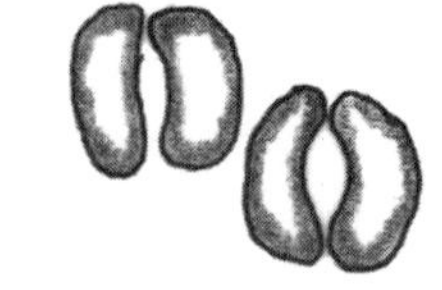

Did You See Me? Tell Your Story! ____________________

____

____

____

DID YOU KNOW? Millions of years ago, my ancestors lived throughout these northern lands. The last one was seen here in 1894, but we were reintroduced in the 1930s. Now, most of us live in herds in cold, northern Alaska.

Muskrat

dzen in Ahtna • Ondatra zibethicus

Hello! I'm Maggie Muskrat, peeking out at you from my favorite plant, the cattail. I love to eat its roots and stems. The ones I don't eat, I combine with rushes, reeds, and other aquatic plants to build my lodge in a marsh, shallow pond, or lake. I pile the vegetation into a conical (CON-i-cul), rounded structure that is at least six feet in diameter and rises three feet above the surface of the water. I enter through an underwater tunnel, the same way my relative, Bernice Beaver, enters her home. In fact, our lodges are very similar, with rooms inside that provide a cozy place to live and to be safe from enemies. What's different about my lodge, though, is that I don't use sticks or wood to build it. I just use small water plants.

In the winter, I build another structure called a "push-up." You see, I'm active all year round, and winter is a dangerous time for me when the ponds freeze and food is difficult to find. So I put together another, smaller mound of water plants, even frozen ones, and build a little ledge inside. This push-up is over a hole in the ice, and, when I swim under the ice, I am able to come right up through the hole that leads into it. This way I have a warm, safe place. But when breakup happens and the ice melts, my push-up falls apart and is gone. That's when I am especially grateful for my sturdy lodge.

Remember I said my lodge looks like Bernice Beaver's? Well, I look like Bernice, and people often think they are seeing her when it is actually me. Our compact bodies are shaped very much alike, and we both have beautiful outer fur with underfur that is soft and warm. We have black, beady eyes, whiskers on our muzzles, and partially webbed feet that make swimming so easy. We have our differences, though, especially in size. She is three times larger than I am, and has a tail that looks like a huge, flat, oval pancake. My tail is long and skinny, and flat on the outside edges. So, if you are by a pond or lake, remember to look for cattails and possibly a ruined pushup pile. Be very still, and I might chatter my teeth or hum for you. I may even swim or splash or dive right in front of you!

My Facts

SIZE:
Body: 10–14 inches long; tail, 8–11 inches long; weight, 2–4 pounds

COLOR:
Body: rich dark to silvery brown
Belly: lighter brown
Tail: dark brown

FOOD:
Omnivorous: roots and stems of cattails, lilies, sedges, grasses, water plants, mussels, shrimp, small fish

DANGERS:
Coyotes, foxes, river otters, mink, owls, humans, winter climate

YEARS I LIVE:
About 3 years

Did You See Me? Tell Your Story! ______________________

____

____

____

DID YOU KNOW? I'm an aquatic rodent who lives south of the Brooks Range in ponds, marshes, and lakes everywhere. Look for large patches of cattails if you want to spot me. Potter's Marsh, near Anchorage, is one of many places I call home.

North American River Otter

sdlagw in Haida • Lutra canadensis

Hi! I'm Olive Otter, trekking along this riverbank. I am a river otter, but I'm also called a land otter. I travel on land to find fresh sources of food when necessary, and I actually move as fast as you do on land. Bet I have more fun, too! I gallop, run, and trot, and, when I come to a muddy hill, I belly-flop and slide on my tummy all the way to the bottom. Even in the winter, my favorite way to get around is by sliding down long, icy hills out onto frozen rivers or lakes. I zoom all over the place! You'll know I've been around if you see my slide marks in the mud or snow.

The majority of my time, though, is spent in the water. I like both fresh water and salt water, and swimming in either is where I feel most at home. My mom taught me to swim when I was only seven weeks old, and it didn't take me long to become a fast, strong, and graceful swimmer. I move through the water as fast as six miles per hour, which is almost the speed you move when you run. You see, I have a very flexible spine which allows my long, sleek body to move in an undulating (UN-due-lay-ting) motion, wiggling up and down rapidly to push myself through the water. Also, my strong, short legs have webbed, back feet that act like paddles. My hindquarters are very muscular, too, which helps my long, thick tail act like a rudder to add more power to my swimming. And if you look closely, you'll notice that I swim with my head slightly under water as well as above water. This allows me to watch for danger on top of the water while I'm swimming just below the surface. We call this submarining. And if danger is near, I dive as deep as sixty feet and stay down for as long as four minutes. I am able to swim more than a quarter of a mile in that amount of time!

I must tell you the truth, though. My life is more play than danger. My family and I are very social, and we hang out with our friends most of the time. We wrestle, play with rocks and sticks, then chase and dunk each other when we are in the water. We even talk to each other in a series of mumbles, barks, grunts, and growls. So if you come and find me, I will tell you what's on my mind!

My Facts

SIZE:
Boar: body, 26–32 inches long, 8–9 inches tall at shoulder; tail, 12–17 inches long; weight, 12–30 pounds
Sow: 25 percent smaller than boar

COLOR:
Back: rich, dark brown or black
Belly: silvery
Throat and chin: grayish

FOOD:
Mainly carnivorous: shellfish, muskrats, crayfish, crab, shrimp, clams, octopi, birds, eggs, insects, some vegetation

DANGERS:
Wolves, coyotes, lynxes, humans

YEARS I LIVE:
8–13 years

Did You See Me? Tell Your Story!

____

____

____

DID YOU KNOW? I am the aquatic member of the weasel family. And because I have a very dense undercoat with longer, thick, guard hairs over top, icy water doesn't bother me. Look for me in water everywhere all year long.

Collared Pika

k'egi in Ahtna • Ochotona collaris

Oh, man. I have GOT to hurry! Petie Pika here, dashing around collecting grasses, stems, twigs, and other tasty greens to add to the big haystack I'm making. See that mound on the ground over there? That's my main haystack, and by the end of summer, it will be two feet tall and two feet across. It's drying in the sun now, but, when winter comes, I'll move the whole thing under the overhang of a boulder so it stays dry. I'm making several smaller stacks, too, in crevices (crev-eh-siz) in the rocks. Since I don't hibernate, I must cache, or store, as much food as possible if I hope to survive the winter. That's why I'm so frantic, trying to build and to guard my stacks.

Yup, I have to guard them. I live in a small colony with several others, and we each have our own half-acre around this rocky slope. My half-acre is supposed to be my very own space, where I have my den in the rocks, haystacks, and enough meadow area below the slope to collect food. Want the truth, though? We all steal from each other. Ugly, but true. In fact, if you listen very carefully, you will hear scolding going on all over the place as we yell at one another to stay away. You might even see me chasing Paulie or Paula or someone else to keep them away from my stacks. This creates a huge problem. I become so focused on protecting my own haystacks and nabbing stuff from others' stacks, I don't even notice when danger is around. Oh, I might accidentally spy an enemy and bark out a shrill warning, but none of us is very alert. What usually saves my hide are the warning whistles and chatters from Maya Marmot and Spike Squirrel, who live in the area and pay much closer attention to danger. When I hear one of them, I know to zoom to the safety of my burrow. If Emma Ermine sneaks in, though, there is no warning. We all stay totally quiet, so she won't know where we are. She's slim enough to slither right down into one of our rock dens. I keep my stocky little body totally still, with my short legs pulled up and my round ears alert to hear where she is going. But she's not here right now, so I must get busy. Think I'll go attack Paulie's haystack. Want to help?

My Facts

SIZE:
Body: 6–8 inches long; tail, 0.5 inch long (not visible); weight, 4–5 ounces

COLOR:
Body: grayish-brown
Chest: white patch
Belly, feet: white
Neck: light collar

FOOD:
Herbivorous: stems, twigs, leaves, grasses, flowers, seeds, forbs

DANGERS:
Weasels, martens, hawks, eagles, owls, parasites

YEARS I LIVE:
3–6 years

Did You See Me? Tell Your Story! ____________________

____

____

____

DID YOU KNOW? I am the only pika in Alaska and have the nickname, "Little Chief Hare." I'm related to hares, but I am much smaller and have little ears. I'm called "collared" because of the grayish fur collar from my ears to my throat.

Common Porcupine

Awta in Sm'algyax • Erethizon dorsatum

Hmph! Hi. My name is Priscilla Porcupine, and I'm a bit prickly. I have about thirty thousand pointy quills covering my body, except on my legs, belly, and the underside of my tail. These hollow, stiff quills are made of keratin (CARE-ah-tin), the same material as your fingernails, and the inside is filled with a thick, lightweight substance. Some quills are short, about two inches long, while others measure over four inches. No matter how long the quill is, you will scream "*OUCH!*" if one pokes you. Quill tips are extremely sharp, and each one has about seven hundred and fifty tiny barbs, or sharp-edged flaps, that overlap each other like fish scales. These barbs point away from the tip, so my quills go into your skin easily, but they are very hard to pull out, just like fishhooks. And my quills move deeper and deeper into your body if you don't take them out, which might make you sick!

I warn you, though, if you come too close. I spray a very stinky odor into the air. It smells like slimy, moldy, rotten cheese. If you don't leave, I grind, smack, and chomp my teeth at you. If you're *still* around, I tighten the skin on my back, making my quills stand straight out. Then I whack my tail on the ground. You need to leave, NOW! But the truth is, I DON'T shoot my quills, and I really DON'T want to fight. In fact, my hollow quills help me float, so if I'm near water, I swim away rather than have a battle with you. My favorite way to escape, though, is to use my long front claws and just go climb up into a tree. I'm actually most at home above the ground, so I spend a great deal of my time high in the branches, either eating or sleeping curled up in a ball.

When I'm not in a tree, it's safer for me to roam around and eat at night, but I do wander in the daytime once in a while. If you look carefully, you might see me waddling down a road, alone, in the morning or late evening. You will know me when you see me: my heavy body, short little legs, small head, long hair, and quills are hard to miss. But remember to keep your distance! I don't want to get under your skin!

My Facts

SIZE:
Boar: body, 18–27 inches long; tail, 7–9 inches long; weight, 20–28 pounds
Sow: 10 percent larger than boar

COLOR:
Back, shoulders: dark guard hairs with yellowish cast
Head, rump, upper surface of tail: yellowish quills
Belly: brown or black (no quills)

FOOD:
Herbivorous: leaves, buds, flowers, and other vegetation in summer; inner bark and layers of trees in winter

DANGERS:
Vehicles, coyotes, wolves, wolverines, foxes, bears, lynxes

YEARS I LIVE:
15–18 years

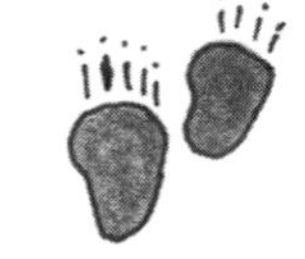

Did You See Me? Tell Your Story! ____________________

____

____

____

DID YOU KNOW? I live along roads in forests and other wooded areas, and I've become the number-one summer road kill. Vehicles are my worst enemy! Other enemies kill me by biting my nose to weaken me, then attacking my quill-less belly.

Dall Sheep

wanadoó in Lingit • Ovis dalli

Hello, there! I'm Shiela Sheep, and I hold two world records. I am the only wild sheep with a pure white coat, and I live farther north than any other wild sheep in the world. Now, I have an interesting question for you. Can you guess how I am like a tree?

Well, you know that trees grow rings, one for every year they have been alive. Count the rings and you know how old the tree is. In the same way, scientists figure out my age by counting the rings in my golden-brown horns. You see, my horns, which are made of keratin (CARE-a-tin), grow quickly in the spring, summer, and early fall, then slow down and stop growing in the winter. As the weather warms, growth begins again. A new ring forms each year, just like a tree.

Speaking of my horns, I must confess that they aren't very big, only about ten inches long, with a slight curve. You know, don't you, that ewes' horns are only a fraction of the size of our rams' horns. Rams all grow massive ones, up to forty inches, curling into a complete, thick circle. It takes at least seven years for their horns to become fully grown, and that's when they begin having battles to prove who is dominant, or stronger. When rams fight, they face each other, stand tall on their hind legs, then charge each other, crashing their huge horns together as hard as they can. The sound is absolutely deafening! And though they don't always inflict serious wounds on each other, I think it's foolish. Life is so dangerous up here, high on the steep slopes, ridges, and rocky crags, why add more trouble?

We spend a lot of time near the timberline, among dangerous, rocky gorges. Our cloven, or split, hooves have rough pads that help us cling to the edges of the steep ledges. We escape most of our enemies because they don't climb and leap as well as we do. Still, our lives are very dangerous. In fact, my lamb, Shelby, is one of the few babies to have survived past three months. Cliffs and predators have taken the rest. Even adults struggle to survive the harsh winters up here, when the snow is deep and food becomes scarce. So when you're near mountains, take a moment to look way up in the crags for white dots. Those might be us!

My Facts

SIZE:
Ram: body, up to 6 feet long, 3 feet tall at shoulder; weight, 250–300 pounds
Ewe: body, up to 5.5 feet long; 2.5 feet tall at shoulder; weight, 150 pounds

COLOR:
Body: white to dirty yellow with age
Hooves: brown or black

FOOD:
Herbivorous: grasses, sedges, lichen, mosses, other plants in summer; woody and frozen plants in winter

DANGERS:
Wolves, coyotes, lynxes, bears, wolverines, humans, deep snow

YEARS I LIVE:
12–15 years

Did You See Me? Tell Your Story!

____

____

____

____

DID YOU KNOW? I live on many of Alaska's mountains, except in Southeast, where there is too much rain and snow for me. In the summer, a great place to spot me is on the Seward Highway above the Windy Corner turnout near Milepost 106.

Masked or Common Shrew

casrarer in Yupik • Sorex cinereus

Um, hello. I'm Scottie Shrew, and I've been elected spokesperson for shrews all over Alaska. There are ten species of us living here, and we have slightly different skulls that only scientists talk about. Also, we live in different places and have varied colorings. We are alike enough, though, that I feel qualified to speak for all of us. Plus, I *am* the most common of all shrews. More of my kind are spread throughout Alaska than any of the others.

The most important information you should remember about us is that we are the smallest mammals that exist anywhere. Honest! Personally, I weigh less than a nickel and am only four inches long, including my tail. I'm a pretty average-sized shrew, so this tells you how tiny we are! Next, you should know that we are insectivores (in-SECT-a-vores), not rodents, which means we eat insects primarily. You might think that since we are so small, we don't need to eat very many bugs. Wrong! If we are awake, we are either eating or trying to find food. In order to stay alive, we must eat more than our body weight of insects every single day. Why, you ask? Well, we are totally hyper and highly energetic, active both day and night. Our hearts beat about one thousand, two hundred times every minute, while yours beats an average of only sixty times a minute. Being this hyper means we must eat continuously.

Because I need so much food, I don't hunt with anyone else. I am a solitary creature, meaning I love to do my own thing and to be on my own. Plus, I don't see well at all, even though my sense of hearing and of smell are outstanding. So if I do see a bug, I don't want someone else grabbing it first. It's hard to be a successful bug hunter when I don't see well!

Now, if your eyesight is better than mine, you will spot me pretty much anywhere in Alaska's forests, tundra, or brushy areas. I will be there, burrowing through grasses and leaves where it is damp and dark. Look carefully for a tiny creature with a long, mouse-like tail, short legs, long whiskers, beady eyes, and of course, my very long, pointed snout, or nose. That snout is the best way to know it's me. Good luck finding me!

My Facts

SIZE:
Body: 2–2.5 inches long; tail, 1.25–2 inches long; weight, 0.1–0.2 of an ounce (weight of a penny to a nickel)

COLOR:
Body: grayish brown
Belly: pale tan
Tail: dark top, light underside

FOOD:
Insectivorous: insects and some small invertebrates

DANGERS:
Weasels, martens, foxes, other small mammals

YEARS I LIVE:
1–1.5 years

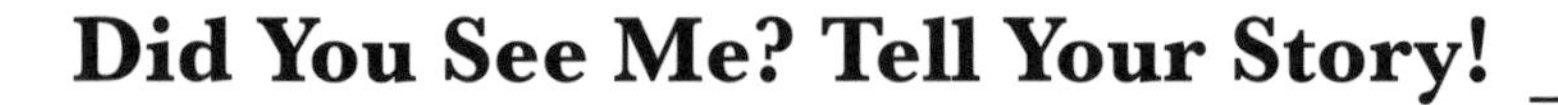

Did You See Me? Tell Your Story! ______________________________

____

____

____

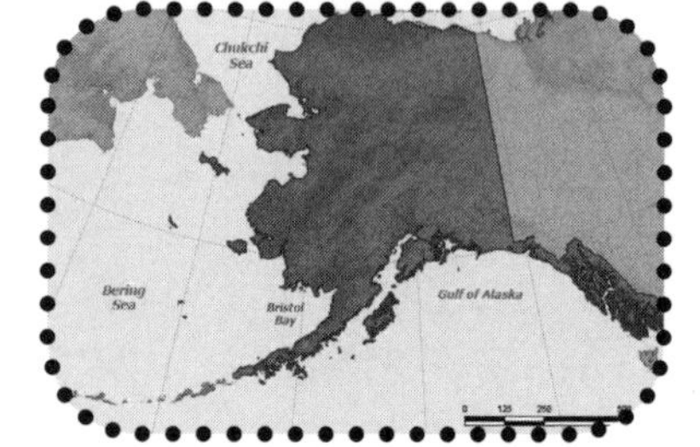

DID YOU KNOW? We build our nests out of dry leaves and grasses inside stumps, under logs, or in piles of brush. Several litters of babies are born every summer, with four to nine in each litter. By one month, babies are on their own.

American Red Squirrel

Desx in Sm'algyax • Tamiasciurus hudsonicus

Oh, my gosh! I have to hurry, hurry, hurry, I have to . . . Oh, hey. I'm Sophie Squirrel, the only tree squirrel in Alaska. From morning 'til night, I rush around trying to fill my midden, or storage area, with as many spruce cones as possible. I love the seeds in these cones, and because I don't hibernate like the others in my family, I have to cache, or store food, for the cold, winter months.

My main midden spreads at the base of this tree, and, over the years, it has grown to be almost three feet deep and twelve feet in diameter. There are many fresh cones in it for next winter, but most of the cluttered mess below is the empty cones and bracts I've dropped over the years while sitting up here, eating seeds. You see, seeds grow inside bracts, or little "leaves" that stick out between the cone's layered scales. I strip the cones of these little bracts, tear them apart, eat the seeds, and drop the rest. This creates a huge pile of trash, but provides a perfect place to cache fresh cones.

This tree, and my favorite branch, are in the middle of my five acres of land that I have stolen successfully over many years. I have several smaller caches and nests throughout my property where I eat and sleep in order to guard my extensive territory. And if I see another of my kind trying to steal from one of my middens or move in on my land, you will hear me before you see me. I bark at intruders with a loud, raucous *chuck-chuck-chuck*, and continue noisy chirps and squeaks until they leave. Sometimes, I even race through the trees and chase them out! That's when I really make a racket. Be aware: I don't share, and I'm NOT social.

When I finally break from my lonely work to rest at night, I snuggle down in one of my nests made of twigs, leaves, and other dried materials. Even on the coldest days in winter, I stay cozy warm in a nest either inside the cavity of a tree or in a "witch's broom," the clump of twigs and sticks that collects in the fork of a spruce tree. But I'm awake most of the time, so listen carefully when you are in the forest, wooded park, or your own backyard. You will hear me chattering as I race through the trees!

My Facts

SIZE:
Body: 6–8 inches long; tail, bushy 5–6 inches long; weight, 6–8 ounces (weight of a medium-sized apple)

COLOR:
Back and sides: summer, deep rusty red with black side stripes; winter, paler rusty gray, no stripes
Belly: whitish
Tail: upper, orange-brown; underside, black-and-yellow grizzled

FOOD:
Omnivorous: spruce cones and seeds, mushrooms, baby snowshoe hares, baby birds, eggs, insects, lichen

DANGERS:
Goshawks, owls, martens, cats

YEARS I LIVE:
5–7 years

Did You See Me? Tell Your Story! ________________________________

____

____

____

DID YOU KNOW? I'm an agile climber who is very curious. If I sneak into your house or cabin, I gnaw on wood, as well as steal fabric and stuffing out of your furniture to use for my nest. I may be cute, but I am destructive.

Arctic Ground Squirrel

qanganaq in Lingit • Spermophilus parryii

Hey there! I'm Spike, your local arctic ground squirrel. Know what else people call me? "Parky" squirrel. Some Alaska Natives use my fur to make parkas, or coats, for both men and women, so they named me parky. You'd think I would get more respect, being the largest of all North American ground squirrels, and the only one in Alaska. I have to admit, though, my fur is good-looking, with the handsome, grizzled, buff-and-gray color on my back and the light cream or rusty color on my belly.

I see why they make coats with me, but I don't like it, and I let them know about it! When I'm being hunted by humans or some other critter, I stand up tall and chatter, making my *sik-sik-sik* sound. I get louder and say more the closer they come. If there is a raptor or other flying predator swooping in close, though, I whistle a shrill warning for all to hear.

It's good to live with others in a colony so we can warn each other when danger is near, especially if Brennen Grizzly is approaching. He loves to eat us, and he doesn't give up. Many times I've had to dive into my den to escape, but the stubborn guy will try to dig me out! If I stay calm and use one of the other exits in my den, I get away from him. But sometimes I panic, lose my head, and just race outside without thinking. He's almost grabbed me several times!

You know, I'm pretty high-strung, which means I get nervous, especially when someone comes into my territory. I don't like intruders, so I become aggressive and upset. I even lose weight over someone coming too near. My normally robust body becomes pretty thin when something in my environment stresses me out. But even then, my body is pretty good looking, with my smooth round head, low rounded ears, blunt nose, and short legs. You may notice that my tail is shorter than other squirrels, and it is only slightly bushy.

Now remember, when you look for me, I live from sea level all the way to the mountains. I like soil that is loose and drains well. Rocky slopes are the best. That's where I make my grass-lined den, and that's where you need to pay very close attention if you want to see me. Listen for my *sik-sik-sik* call or my shrill scream!

My Facts

SIZE:
Body: 9–14 inches long; tail, 3–6 inches long; weight, 1.5–2.5 pounds

COLOR:
Back and sides: grizzled brown, gray, and buff
Belly: buff or white to rusty
Feet, legs: light cream
Tail: brown-and-black-flecked

FOOD:
Omnivorous: seeds, bulbs, grass stems and roots, mushrooms, eggs, insects, small vertebrates, carrion

DANGERS:
Brown bears, foxes, wolverines, lynxes, weasels, raptors, humans

YEARS I LIVE:
6–10 years

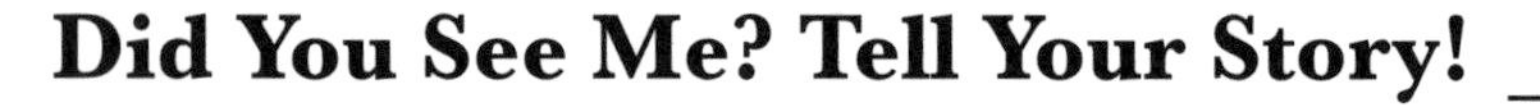

Did You See Me? Tell Your Story! ______________________

____

____

____

DID YOU KNOW? In the winter, I hibernate in the sleeping chamber of my den. My body temperature falls as low as twenty-eight degrees for a few weeks; then I warm up for a time; and then I get very cold again. Winter is difficult!

Northern Red-Backed Vole

Ugna'aq in Sugpiaq • Clethrionuomys rutilus

I'm Vinnie Vole, and I can't talk for very long. If I don't keep moving, someone will eat me. I'm serious! I'm just a small, fuzzy-coated, mouse-sized rodent with big ears and a very short, pointed tail. I wish it wasn't true, but I am the staple, or main food, of most of Alaska's carnivores, those critters who eat meat. I am on almost every land mammals' menu in the state.

How do I survive? Well, I'm hunted by someone day and night, so I venture out to look for my food only during twilight, at dawn or dusk. It's harder to see me then. Also, my kind is difficult to find because our coat blends in with the colors of the terrain where we live. That's an adaptation, or change, that happened slowly over many years. My relatives living on the tundra have pale fur that matches the lighter flora, or plant life, of that area. I live in the taiga (TA-ja), or coniferous (con-NIF-er-ous) forest, so I have a darker, reddish-brown coat to help me hide in the dark woods.

Now, you know that I don't hibernate, right? In order to survive in the snow, I tunnel through it. I move as quickly through snow as I do through the leaves and twigs that cover the ground the rest of the year. My survival depends on being able to move fast! And survival for our babies is a huge challenge because they don't move quickly at all. Our females have several litters of three to nine babies during the spring and summer, and from the minute those young ones are born, they are in serious danger. Sophie Squirrel, that wild red squirrel, is especially crazy about them, jumping and jiving all over the place when she finds a litter. We try so hard to hide our elaborate, grass-lined nests under rocks, logs, and other shelters on the ground so Sophie doesn't find them. But she searches until she locates her meal, and more than half of our little ones don't survive past a few weeks.

Personally, I have more hope for survival if I stay alone or just with my immediate family. A large colony draws too much attention. And speaking of that, if I stand here talking any more, I will be somebody's next meal. So watch for me zooming under bushes or darting across a road. I'll be speeding!

My Facts

SIZE:
Body: 4 inches long; tail, 1.5 inches long; weight, 1–1.5 ounces (6–9 quarters)

COLOR:
Back: rusty red with a center stripe
Sides: gray-brown
Belly: tannish
Tail: brown on top, light underside, black tip

FOOD:
Omnivorous: grasses, berries and other fruits, seeds, lichen, fungi, insects, carrion

DANGERS:
Red squirrels, weasels, martens, foxes, coyotes, owls, hawks, birds, other voles, fish

YEARS I LIVE:
1–2 years

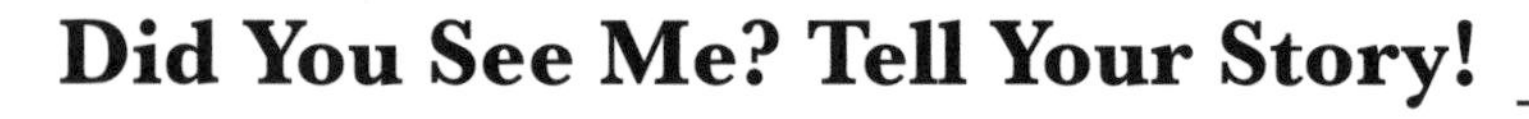

Did You See Me? Tell Your Story!

DID YOU KNOW? There are seven species of voles in Alaska, and we live in almost every area of the state. I look like a regular old mouse except for my tiny, pointed tail. I am a terrific swimmer, so watch for me in ponds and lakes.

Gray Wolf

Gyibaaw in Sm'algyax • Canis lupus

My Facts

SIZE:
Dog: body, 4–5 feet long; tail, 14–19 inches long; weight, 85–150 pounds
She-wolf: 10–15 percent smaller than dog

COLOR:
Body: varies from pure black to all white with gray, tan, brown, and yellow mixtures
Legs, underside: off-white or cream
Tail: often black-tipped

FOOD:
Carnivorous: moose, elk, caribou, deer, sheep, goats, small mammals, salmon, each other

DANGERS:
Other wolves, brown bears, humans

YEARS I LIVE:
10–16 years

Hey! Worthington Wolf here with a couple of boys from my pack. There's a caribou herd at the bottom of this hill, and a large doe is hanging back with her newborn calf. We're going to take them both down. I don't hunt alone when it's a large critter, especially one with a youngster. So I just gave a howl-out to rally more of my pack and to let them know where we are. We'll move in together, surround the pair, then easily make our kill.

I don't hunt and eat every day, and it's been a few days since my last meal. I will probably put away fifteen pounds or more of this caribou, as will some of the others in my pack. Any leftovers might be buried, like dogs do with bones, or we could decide to leave the scraps for the ravens who always follow us. I am the alpha, or lead, male, and my mate is the alpha female. We are the oldest members of the pack, and its leaders. All decisions are made by my mate or me, and the others never question our choices.

Right now, there are eleven in our pack. Some of the six pups from last year will leave soon, but if they aren't ready, they'll stay longer. Three of our older pups are still with us now. We all live together on our established territory of about nine hundred square miles. This land covers the biggest range of any land mammal, and having plenty of space is necessary for us. We are rather shy and nervous around others and adequate space is important. We can be happy on all types of terrain, as long as we find food.

Now I want you to be very aware that I am protective of my pack. Extremely so. My easy pace of five miles per hour changes to a fast forty miles per hour if I need to chase off, or kill, an intruder. Moose, deer, any creature at all—it becomes our meal if we are hungry. So, if you happen onto my land and see me, don't come close. Even though I'm related to your pet dog at home, and might even look like him, know this: I am the largest of the wild dogs, and I am not tame. Never will I be your best friend nor walk on a leash. I represent the spirit of the wilderness, and *I am wild! Yeoowwllll!*

Did You See Me? Tell Your Story! ____________________

____

____

____

DID YOU KNOW? I am often seen and heard in Denali National Park. Your author saw me trot right up to the door of the camper bus that she was riding into the park. It was incredibly exciting for everyone, including me!

Wolverine

naltsiis in Ahtna • Gulo gulo

Do I look like I'm snarling? You had better believe I am! Woodruff Wolverine here, and I have a reputation to uphold. My name means "glutton," and my nickname is "devil bear." These are accurate descriptions as I am a fierce, vicious beast who resembles a small bear with a bushy tail. I am a glutton, an opportunistic omnivore who eats anything and everything I find. I gorge myself on meat, dead or alive, fill in with plants, and spend my life scavenging for food. I lope or gallop as fast as thirty miles per hour to chase down and catch Scottie Shrew or Farley Fox. I even chase Sophie Squirrel into her tree with the help of my long, sharp, curved claws that are great for climbing. I eat like a complete pig when I find Wilma Whale washed up on the beach. Even Mortimer Moose is in trouble if he's trapped in deep snow.

I do prefer dead critters or leftovers from someone else's meal, so I don't have to work as hard. In fact, when I find Worthington Wolf or Brennen Bear on their kill, I've been known to chase them away from their prey and finish eating it for them. And I steal dead varmints from trap lines, then take the trapper's own food if I find it. I love to eat and stop at nothing to secure food!

Now, in the winter, my muscular, low-slung body, short legs, and huge feet help me move quickly through the snow. The elements don't slow me down, but many critters hibernate. Live food is difficult to find, so I eat frozen meat. A whole beast or old, messy scraps frozen into the snow—I'm not choosey. My jaw and neck muscles are so strong that I crush and eat every part of my meal, including hides, hooves, and bones. I don't always find food, though, and starvation is possible. To be sure I survive, I hunt day and night, wandering up to thirty miles a day, all year long. I stay on my home range that includes hundreds of square miles of undisturbed wilderness. My range might be in taiga and boreal (BORE-re-el) forests, on the tundra, high in the mountains, or along the beach. Terrain doesn't matter as long as there is food. And if you show up, I'm gone. Your kind wants my fur to trim coats, so I become the hunted. That ain't happenin'!

My Facts

SIZE:
Wolverine: body, 28–34 inches long, 12–18 inches tall at shoulder; tail, 7–10 inches long; weight, 30–55 pounds
Angeline: 30 percent smaller than wolverine

COLOR:
Body: dark brown to black with two light side-stripes from shoulder to rump
Neck, chest: white patch
Head: grizzled gray

FOOD:
Omnivorous: consumes everything found

DANGERS:
Wolves, bears, humans

YEARS I LIVE:
4–7 years

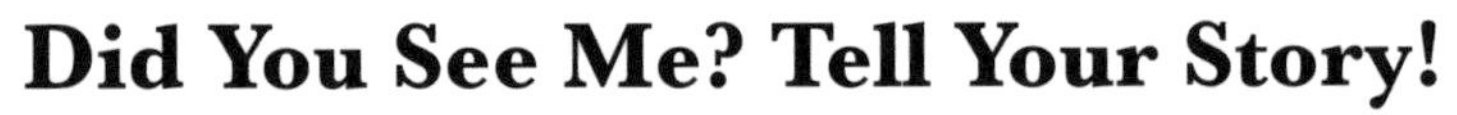

DID YOU KNOW? In February or March, our females build dens in snow caves or under rocks. That is where they have one to five kits, or babies. I make my den for sleeping in any place that is sheltered from the rain and snow.

Woodchuck

gwi łgw in Haida • Marmota monax

I'm Whitney Woodchuck, but if you hear someone shout, "Hey, there's a groundhog!" or, "That's a whistle-pig!" or, "See that land beaver?" they are just using a different name for the same critter . . . me! No matter what you call me, though, I'm not going to be easy to spot.

You know about Groundhog Day on the first Monday of February? That's when Punxsutawney Phil, the world's most famous groundhog, or woodchuck, comes out of his den in Pennsylvania to look for his shadow. If he sees it, there are supposed to be six more weeks of winter. Well, I don't wake up or come out of my den here in Alaska until April or May, and the further north I live, the longer I sleep. You see, I'm a true hibernator, meaning when it's cold, I sleep. My body temperature, breathing, heart rate, and body functions slow way down, and I go into a state of torpor (TOR-pur), or total inactivity. Alone in my burrow, with all the tunnels plugged, I sleep from October until it warms up in the spring. This means you only have about six months to try to find me, so you need to look carefully and quickly.

I hang out in grassy or dry woodland areas, near spruce forests with low undergrowth, or even in rocky ravines. Watch for a large, brownish-red rodent with a heavy body, short, broad head, beady eyes, and small, rounded ears. My long, bushy tail should tell you that I am part of the squirrel family. In fact, you might mistake me for Spike, my arctic squirrel cousin, who sits up tall the way I do. I'm larger and chubbier than Spike, though, and bigger than dainty Sophie Red Squirrel.

Now, a good way to find me is to look for our colony, where we each have our own territory containing a mounded den. You will see dirt piles all over the place that come from kicking soil to the surface as we make our extensive tunnels and burrows. I love to sit up tall right next to my very own dirt pile.

But truth be told, I'm not very social, and I stay away from my neighbors. We do share lookout duty, though, and screech a loud, shrill whistle when danger is near. That's why I'm called a "whistle-pig." So if you want to see me, come when I'm awake and don't let me see you first. I'll be gone in a whistle and a flash!

My Facts

SIZE:
Body: 16–20 inches long; tail, 3–7 inches long; weight, 5–10 pounds (lighter after hibernation)

COLOR:
Body: frosted, reddish-brown
Belly: light brown
Face: brown
Feet: dark brown to black

FOOD:
Herbivorous: grasses, flowering plants, berries, roots, mosses, lichen, insects, eggs

DANGERS:
Foxes, hawks, weasels, owls, humans, dogs

YEARS I LIVE:
3–5 years

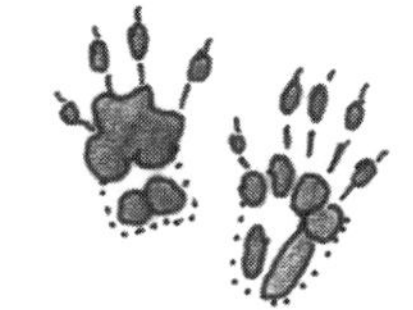

Did You See Me? Tell Your Story! ______________________

____

____

____

DID YOU KNOW? When I need to escape danger, I scamper into my den, if it is close. In the forest, I race up trees easily with my strong, sharp claws. And if I'm near water, I dive right in and swim like a fish to evade my enemy.

What Kind of Bear Is It?

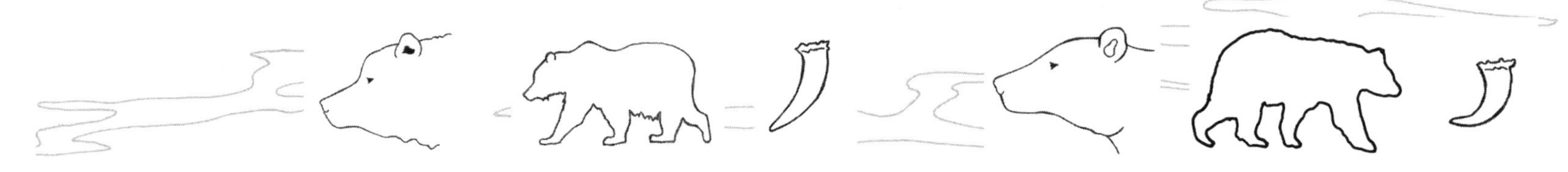

Coastal and Grizzly Brown Bears	Black Bear
Higher at shoulder when viewed from side	Higher at rump when viewed from side
Prominent hump over shoulder	No hump
Large, round head	Small head with wide forehead
Round, dish-shaped face	Long, straight nose
Massive body	Smaller body
Burly and strong	Less muscular
Long, slightly curved claws	Short, obviously curved claws

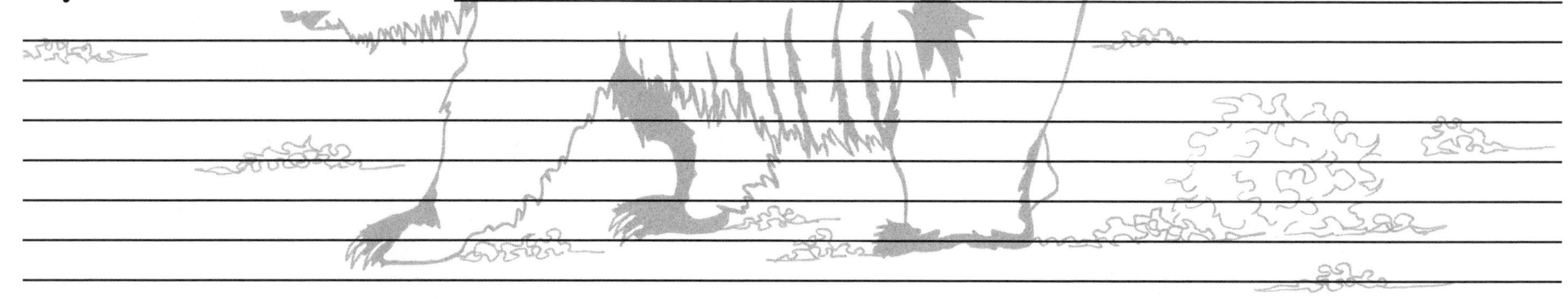

My Notes about Bears:

Bear Safety

Be bear aware! Watch for warning signs posted by trailheads, campgrounds, and other places. Look for evidence of bears: scat (poop), tracks, or fur caught on a bush. Watch, listen, and be aware of the smells around you. Bears give off a strong odor.

Never approach a bear for any reason. Usually bears will avoid humans. Make noise, sing, clap your hands, wear bear bells, or talk loudly so you don't surprise a bear. A bear near food, fish, or dead prey is extremely dangerous. Also, a mother bear with cubs is intensely protective of her young. Stay far away!

Never run from a bear. They may think you are an animal and chase you. You cannot outrun a bear!

If you see a bear and it has not seen you . . .

Be very quiet and back away slowly, watching the bear at all times. Know where it is.

When you no longer see the bear, move quickly out of the area.

Report your sighting to a ranger or the Department of Fish and Game.

If you see a bear and it sees you . . .

Stand your ground and face the bear.

Talk calmly to the bear to let it know you are human, then back slowly away, staying clear of the route or path the bear is taking.

If you are with others, stand close together in one group and try to look big by waving your arms over your heads.

If attacked by a bear . . .

Identify what kind of bear it is. The differences between a brown bear and a black bear are on the previous page.

If it's a brown bear, play dead.

Immediately lie facedown on the ground, grasp your hands behind your neck to protect it, and spread your legs widely so the bear cannot turn you over.

If the bear leaves, stay there until you are sure it has left the area.

If the attack continues, fight back. Kick, punch, hit the face, eyes, and nose—do everything you can to hurt it and to get away.

If the attacking bear is a black bear, do NOT play dead.

Immediately fight back by hitting the bear as hard as you can.

Black bears do not leave if you appear non-threatening. You need to fight as hard as you can to free yourself and leave the area.

Moose Safety

With their odd way of walking, big nose, huge antlers, and strange dewlap, moose are entertaining to watch. But moose are wild animals and very dangerous, especially cows with calves. More people are injured every year by moose than by bears, so be aware of ways to be safe around moose.

Remember: Moose are not tame, do not like to be petted, and will hurt you if they are upset or threatened.

If you see a moose and it does not see you . . .

Quietly and quickly move away until you no longer see it. NEVER, EVER approach or go up to a moose.

If the moose sees you . . .

Pay attention to its body language. If it is watching you, with its ears straight up, it is wondering what you are doing. It is not ready to charge, and you are safe to move away immediately.

If the moose's ears are laid back, the fur on its neck is up, or it paws the ground, it may be ready to charge. If there is a large rock, tree, or other solid object near you, move behind it immediately. Run to safety as soon as you can.

It is all right to run away from a moose.

Unlike a bear, a moose will not chase you, or if it does, it will stop almost immediately once you have left the area.

If the moose charges you and knocks you down . . .

Lie on the ground, curl up in a ball, and protect your head with your arms. Be still until the moose leaves, then quickly run to safety.

Common Land Mammal Families

Bat	*Bear*	*Cat*	*Cattle*	*Deer*
bat	black	lynx	bison	caribou
	coastal brown		goat	deer
	grizzly brown		muskox	elk
			sheep	moose

Dog	*Hare Form*	*Rodent*	*Shrew Form*	*Weasel*
coyote	hare	beaver	shrew	ermine
fox	pika	lemming		martin
wolf	rabbit (no wild rabbits live in Alaska)	marmot		mink
		muskrat		otter
		porcupine		wolverine
		squirrel		
		vole		
		woodchuck		

Glossary

alder: a type of tree that grows in wet ground (a thicket is a large group of these trees)

alluvial plain: large, flat area of land formed by sand, clay, and gravel deposited when a river floods and recedes

bracts

alpine meadow: a meadow high in the mountains filled with low grasses

barren land: land with poor soil, lots of sand, and rocks, where plants grow poorly

boreal forest: cold, wet area in the far north where conifer trees grow (see *taiga*)

bract: special small leaf in the cones of trees important for seed development

carnivore: an animal who eats only meat *carnivorous*: one who eats only meat

conifers: trees that stay green all year and have cones, needles, or flat, scaled leaves

crags: steep, narrow rugged peaks in the mountains

estuary

estuary: where the fresh water of a river connects with the saltwater ocean, often called the "mouth of a river"

forbs: flowering plants with leaves or seeds, but not a grass

guard hairs: long, coarse outer hairs that cover soft underfur on some mammals, including the muskox

herbivore: an animal who eats only plants

herbivorous: describes one who eats only plants

insectivore: an animal who eats only insects

insectivorous: describes one who eats insects

invertebrates: animals with no backbone, such as jellyfish, snails, and octopi

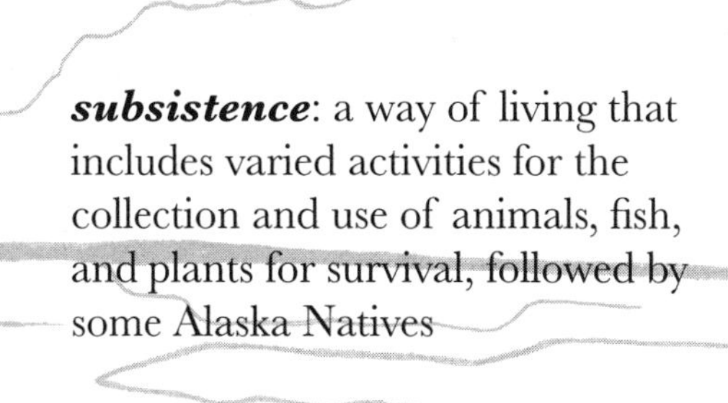

keratin: main material in fingernails, hair, antlers, horns, and baleen

omnivore: an animal who eats both plants and animals

caribou

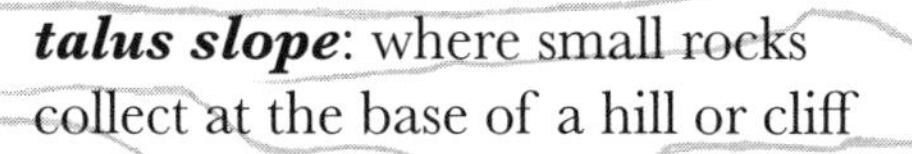

omnivorous: describes one who eats both plants and animals

pelage: coat of fur on an animal

permafrost: ground under the topsoil that is frozen most of the year

sedges: grass-like plants or bushes

shovels: large, flat, curved areas on caribou antlers

spawn: when salmon swim upriver to lay their eggs

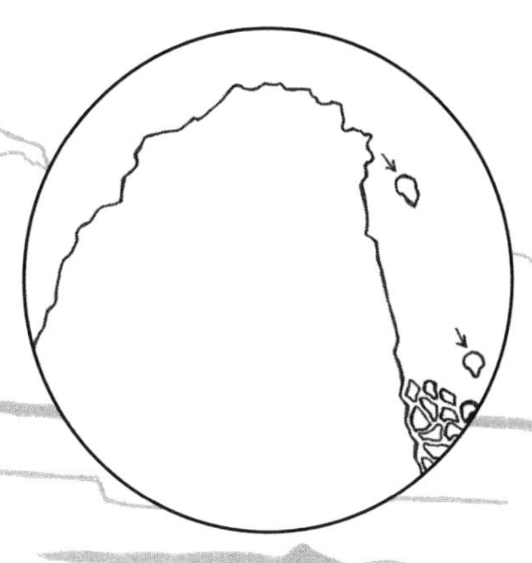

talus slope

subsistence: a way of living that includes varied activities for the collection and use of animals, fish, and plants for survival, followed by some Alaska Natives

talus slope: where small rocks collect at the base of a hill or cliff

taiga: moist, coniferous forest in far northern Alaska, beginning where the tundra ends

tufts

terrain: physical features of an area of land, such as smooth, flat, hilly, or rocky

tufts: fur that stands up on the top of a lynx's ears and looks like narrow feathers

tundra: inland, flat, treeless arctic region where the ground is usually frozen below the surface

Learn More About the Mammals of Alaska

Places to see a variety of mammals:

Alaganik Slough Trail, Milepost 17, Copper River Highway

Alaska Sea Life Center, Seward

Alaska Wildlife Conservation Center near the Portage turnoff

Alaska Zoo, Anchorage

Chugach State Park, Eagle River/Anchorage

Denali National Park

Kenai Spur Highway and Kenai River Viewing Platforms, Soldotna/Kenai

Kincaid Park, Anchorage

Moose Pond, Lost Lake Trail

Muskox Farm, Palmer

Potter Marsh, Anchorage

Reindeer Farm, Palmer

Richardson Highway between Paxson and Delta Junction (bison)

Sterling Highway, Milepost 106, Windy Corner turnout (Dall sheep)

Places to see bears:

McNeil River Game Sanctuary (permit only)

Katmai National Park

Russian River Falls out of Russian River Campground, Milepost 52 on Sterling Highway

Hidden Creek near Skilak Lake

Salmon Creek near Hyder

Kodiak Island

Chilkoot Lake State Park

Numerous fly-in opportunities

Online:

Alaska Department of Fish and Game website for all animals: http://www.adfg.alaska.gov/index.cfm?adfg=animals.listall

National Oceanic and Atmospheric Administration for kids: http://oceanservice.noaa.gov/kids/

http://www.kidzone.ws/animals/mammals.htm

Further reading:

Alaska Mammals, Alaska Geographic

Alaska's Mammals, by Dave Smith and Tom Walker

Mammals of Alaska, Alaska Geographic Guides

The Nature of Alaska: A Waterford Press Field Guide

Peterson's Field Guides to Mammals of North America

Whalewatcher, by Trevor Day